INSPIRATIONAL *Short Stories* ABOUT SUCCESS *and* HAPPINESS

Insightful Words of Wisdom to Uplift the Heart and Reawaken the Spirit

Complied by:
Verusha Singh and Virend Singh

Copyright 2016 by Ink 'n Ivory Pty Ltd All rights reserved.

Published by
Ink 'n Ivory
P O Box 6321, Rouse Hill, NSW. 2155. Australia

www.inkNivory.com
Printed in Australia

First Printing: 2016
ISBN: 978-1-922113-19-1 (Paperback)
ISBN: 978-1-922113-20-7 (Mobi)
ISBN: 978-1-922113-21-4 (ePub)

Disclaimer
This publication is shared with the understanding that the publisher and author are not engaged in rendering financial, psychological or any other professional service and is offered for information purposes only. If financial or any other professional advice or assistance is required, the services of a competent professional person should be sought. The reader is solely responsible for his/ her own actions arising from the use of this document.

Contents

FREE DOWNLOAD

Get "ACCELERATED GOAL ACHIEVEMENT: AN AUTHENTIC APPROACH TO SET AND ACHIEVE GOALS FASTER" for free!

Go to:

www.TheInexplicableLawsOfSuccess.com/free-goal-book/

Introduction

Everyone, at some point in their lives, feels overwhelmed by the challenges and obstacles that they have to face. In times of difficulty, we often look around to find a source of inspiration and hope. Sometimes the easiest and most powerful way to get a message across is through a story. Stories hold our attention and stay with us long after we have heard them. *Inspirational Short Stories about Success and Happiness* will inspire and uplift you with its stories of optimism, faith, and strength.

The Secret to Creating Affluence

This beautiful fable illustrates the mystifying and sometimes illusive nature of the Law of Cause and Effect.

A young man went to the forest and said to his spiritual master, 'I want to have unlimited wealth, to help and heal the world. What is the secret to wealth?'

The spiritual master said, 'There are two Goddesses that reside in the heart of every human being: the Goddess of WEALTH and the Goddess of KNOWLEDGE'.

'Although you love both, you must pursue one of them to the exclusion of the other. Pursue her, love her, and give her your attention. Understand that only the Goddess of Wealth can give you wealth, and you may pursue only one Goddess, not both'.

'But, here is the secret: If you pursue the Goddess of Wealth, she will be pleased with you because she loves to be chased. The more you pursue her the more she will elude you. However, if you pursue the Goddess of KNOWLEDGE, the Goddess of WEALTH will become extremely jealous and pay more attention to you. In fact, the more you seek the Goddess of Knowledge, the more the Goddess of Wealth will seek you. She will never leave you. She will constantly shower you with material blessings just to win your attention, and the wealth you desire will be yours forever'.

Adapted from (Chopra, 1993)

Ponder this:

The human tendency is to pursue the Goddess of Wealth, which seems like the logical choice. However, wealth is simply an effect, and like any effect it has a cause. In the fable, pursuing one goddess gets you the best of both worlds; wealth comes from the acquisition and proper application of knowledge.

Your "Mystical" Mind

Claire, a former professional dancer, was 47 and dying from a disease called primary pulmonary hypertension when, in 1988, she had a pioneering heart-lung transplant in America. After she recovered from the operation, she suddenly had a craving for beer and KFC (Kentucky Fried Chicken). She was baffled because she had never before desired either. According to her teenage daughter, she even began walking like a man. Months after the operation, she began having mysterious dreams about a young man named Tim. She tracked down the donor of her new organs and learnt that they had come from Timothy, the victim of a fatal motorcycle accident. When she contacted his family, the woman was stunned to discover that he did have a particular fondness for drinking beer and eating KFC.

(Sylvia, 2008)

Ponder this:

The remarkable thing about this story is that the lady had a heart-lung transplant, NOT a brain transplant! So the information about the beer and KFC had to be stored in the cells of the heart and lungs which she received from Tim. Fascinating, isn't it? This suggests that information is stored in every cell of our body and not only in the brain or mind!

The Devil's Best Tool

One day the devil decided that God had received too much good publicity and he too deserved some publicity for the work he does to make this world an interesting place. He called a major TV news network and, after identifying himself, arranged an interview.

For the interview, he transported the reporter and the camera crew to Hell and gave them a tour of a strange sort of art gallery. His gallery did not consist of elements of great art. Instead, his gallery was made up of a number of rooms of varying sizes, each one dedicated to a specific item of interest. In one room were piles of gold on a marble table, stacked to the ceiling. 'This is my greed room', the devil said. 'Greed is one of my favourite tools.'

Moving to the second room, the devil showed the reporter and camera crew a group of men and women enjoying themselves in a cocktail lounge at a convention. 'This is my infidelity room', the devil said. 'This is a place of temptation to the person who is far away from home.'

The devil continued in this manner, proudly presenting rooms with addictive drugs, alcohol, firearms, weapons and other destructive items.

Finally, the camera crew came to the last room. The devil paused and said, 'Herein lies my greatest tool. With this tool, I can accomplish more evil than with all the other tools at my disposal, put together.'

Keen to see the contents of this room, the camera crew and the reporter moved closer to the door as the devil opened it triumphantly. In the room was a small item on a pedestal positioned in the beam of a spotlight.

At first glance, it appeared to be a seemingly harmless wedge-shaped object. Curiously, the camera crew edged closer to the object, only to find that it was a simple wedge — similar to a common doorstop.

Bewildered how this could be his greatest tool, they turned and looked at the devil enquiringly as if to ask 'What in hell is this?'. The devil smiled and said, 'This is the wedge of self-doubt. With it, I can shatter a person's self-image. I drive this wedge in the back of a person's mind between their abilities and their possibilities. If I create a gap between someone's abilities and what is truly possible for them, then I can completely destroy that person. In fact, I use this tool every day to destroy millions of lives.'

It's true, even the slightest doubt can stop you dead in your tracks. Indeed, it is what stops most people in their tracks thereby robbing them of a better life

Adapted from various versions on the internet.

Ponder this:

Doubt keeps us from making positive and long-lasting changes in our lives. Many of us have tiny cracks in our self-image and when we allow ourselves or other people to drive the 'wedge of doubt' into those cracks, we set ourselves up for catastrophic failure.

You Are Divine

A Hindu legend aptly describes the divine power inherent in each of us.

There was a time when men were gods. But they abused their divine powers so much that Lord Brahma, the master of all gods, decided to take these powers away and hide them in a place where they would be impossible to find.

The lesser gods debated the issue of the hiding place. They suggested: 'Why not bury man's powers in the earth?' Lord Brahma replied, 'No, that will not do because man would dig deep and find them.'

Then the gods said, 'We will send their divinity to the deepest depths of the ocean.'

But Lord Brahma replied again, 'Sooner or later man will explore the depths of the ocean and he will find those powers and bring them to the surface.'

The lesser gods concluded, 'Neither land nor sea is a place where man's divine powers will be safely hidden. Therefore there is no place to hide them.'

At that moment Lord Brahma exclaimed, 'This is what we will do with man's divinity! We will hide it deep within him because that is the only place he will not think to look.'

From then on, according to the legend, man searched the world over; he explored, climbed, dove and dug in search of something that was inside himself the whole time.

(Baba, 2005)

Ponder this:

It is also written that people are created in the same image and likeness of God. You might be familiar with the following quote:

Ye are Gods and the spirit of God dwells within you.

– Corinthians 3:16

What this means is that *you are divine*. You've always been and always will be. Your soul is the individualised essence of God.

The Unsolvable Math Problem

One day in 1939, George Bernard Dantzig, a doctoral candidate at the University of California, Berkeley, arrived late for a graduate-level statistics class and found two problems written on the board. He quickly copied the two math problems on the board, assuming that they were the homework assignment. It took him several days to work through the two problems, but he finally completed them. The next day he dropped the homework on the professor's desk.

On a Sunday morning a few days later, George was awakened early by a call from his excited professor. Since George had been late for that class, he hadn't heard the professor announce that the two problems on the board were mathematical mind-teasers that even Einstein hadn't been able to solve. But George Dantzig, believing that he was working on ordinary homework problems, had solved not one, but two problems that had stumped mathematicians for hundreds of years!

(Kersey, 1998)

Ponder this:

When people are allowed to pursue goals free from presumed limitations on what they can accomplish, they just may manage some extraordinary feats through the combined application of natural talent and hard work.

The Hundredth Monkey Phenomenon

The Japanese monkey, Macaca fuscata, had been observed in the wild for a period of over thirty years.

In 1952, on the island of Koshima, scientists were providing monkeys with sweet potatoes dropped in the sand. The monkeys liked the taste of the raw sweet potatoes, but they found the dirt unpleasant. An 18-month-old female (named Imo) found she could get rid of the sand by washing the potatoes in a nearby stream. She taught this trick to her mother and her playmates; they taught their mothers, too.

This cultural innovation was gradually picked up and between 1952 and 1958 all the young monkeys learned to wash the sandy sweet potatoes to make them more palatable. Only the adults who imitated their children learned this social improvement. Other adults kept eating the dirty sweet potatoes.

One day in 1958, something interesting happened. A certain number of Koshima monkeys were washing sweet potatoes. The exact number is not known. Let's assume that there were 99 monkeys washing potatoes. Let's further assume that later that morning, the hundredth monkey learned to wash potatoes.

Then a most amazing phenomenon occurred!

By that evening almost every monkey in the tribe was washing sweet potatoes before eating them. The added energy of this hundredth monkey somehow created an ideological breakthrough!

But, it didn't end there. A most surprising thing observed by these scientists was that the monkeys' habit of washing sweet potatoes then jumped across the sea.

Colonies of monkeys on other islands and the mainland troop of monkeys at Takasakiyama began washing their sweet potatoes too!

Thus, when a certain critical number achieve an awareness, this new awareness may be communicated from mind to mind. Although the exact number may vary, this Hundredth Monkey Phenomenon means that when only a limited number of people know of a new way, it may remain the conscious property of these people. But, there is a point at which, if only one more person tunes-in to a new awareness, an energy field is strengthened so that this awareness is picked up by almost everyone!

(The Hundredth Monkey Phenomenon, 2009)

Ponder this:

It's a remarkable story that illustrates how information can be transmitted across physical boundaries and almost magically become embraced by individuals or groups without them even being aware of it! Everything is energy; we are an integral part of this matrix of universal energy; we are connected to everything else in existence.

A Student's Quest for Success

A student went to his spiritual teacher and said, 'Guru, I want to experience success. How can I become successful quickly?' The teacher smiled and said, 'All right, I'll teach you the secret of success. Meet me at the Ganges River at 5:00 am tomorrow.'

The next morning the student showed up at 5:00 am at the appointed place only to find his teacher already bathing in the river. The teacher beckoned the student to come into the water and join him. Keen to learn the secret of success, the student obeyed the teacher without question.

The teacher then put his hand on the student's head and firmly held it under the water. Gasping for air, the student struggled to get out, but the teacher maintained his grip keeping him under the water for more than a minute. The teacher knew the precise moment he had to release his grip on the student. Coughing up water that he had swallowed, the student angrily demanded, 'Why did you do that?

The teacher then said, 'Before I answer your question, tell me: what were you thinking of under the water? What was it that you were looking for? Success? Status? Wealth?'

'None of that, sir. I desperately wanted air. Nothing, but air.'

The teacher then said, 'If you want success in your life as

desperately as you wanted that breath of air, then you will have it — and as quickly as you want.'

Adapted from various versions on the internet.

Ponder this:

You can tell how badly you want to achieve a goal by observing your actions each day. When you have a burning desire for something, you will do whatever it takes to make it happen. If you don't have a "Damn the torpedoes, Full speed ahead!" attitude, it's an indication you don't want it badly enough.

Snapshot at Lourdes

Carol Anderson was a young widow whose husband had died of cancer at thirty-five. Bob Edwards was a young widower whose wife had been killed in a car accident at twenty-nine. Both marriages had been extremely happy, and both Carol and Bob were sure they would never love or marry again. After many lonely years of pain and suffering, they met at a church dinner and started courting. When they got engaged and then married, they told everyone that it was miraculous that they had found each other. Their relationship was strong and loving. The only trouble spot in the marriage was that they had diametrically different opinions on what to do about the past.

Carol longed to bury it; Bob needed to explore it. Carol never wanted to talk about either of their previous marriages. Bob, on the other hand, was eager to know the minutest details of Carol's life before they had met, and was hurt that Carol showed such a complete lack of interest in his.

'Why raise ghosts?' Carol would ask when Bob would persist with his gentle probing and soft inquiries.

'Memory should be preserved, not obliterated,' he would reply. This went on for years, with Carol's perspective ultimately prevailing. As a result they never shared stories, pictures, or mementos from their first marriages.

Ten years later, Carol felt their marriage was secure enough to withstand any assaults from the past. 'Okay,' she told Bob one day, 'I'm ready to talk.' She began telling Bob about her first marriage and pulled out several snapshots albums she had hidden from him all these years. 'These are from our honeymoon,' she said, starting to leaf through the pages of one album. 'We went to France. Oh, here we are at Lourdes.

'You went to Lourdes?' Bob said with mild interest. 'So did we.'

'Well, I guess half the world goes to Lourdes,' Carol laughed. 'No big deal. Everyone was looking for blessings and miracles in their lives.'

'Wait a second, Carol, turn back a page,' said Bob suddenly. 'Let me see the snapshot again of you and Ralph at Lourdes.'

Carol obligingly turned back a page.

'Carol," her husband asked tensely, 'who is that couple in the background?'

'I have no idea,' she said. 'Just as the photographer snapped the picture, a couple walked by and got caught by the shutter. I can see why you asked, though, thinking they were with us. In the picture it does look as though they're standing behind us, almost as if they're posing, but it's just an illusion.'

'You're wrong, Carol,' Bob said slowly. 'It wasn't a mistake, it was destiny. You see that couple in the background was me and my first wife.'

(Halberstam and Leventhal, 1997)

Ponder this:

When events like this happen, it can certainly make you wonder about the concepts of destiny and free will. Nothing about your life is casual or per chance. Things happen for a reason even if they appear spooky in the way they show up.

The Power of Giving

It was a really hot summer's day many years ago. I was on my way to pick up two items at the grocery store. In those days, I was a frequent visitor to the supermarket because there never seemed to be enough money for a whole week's food-shopping at once.

You see, my young wife, after a tragic battle with cancer, had died just a few months earlier. There was no insurance, just many expenses and a mountain of bills. I held a part-time job, which barely generated enough money to feed my two young children.

Things were bad, really bad.

And so it was that day, with a heavy heart and four dollars in my pocket, I was on my way to the supermarket to purchase a gallon of milk and a loaf of bread. The children were hungry and I had to get them something to eat. As I came to a red traffic light, I noticed on my right a young man, a young woman and a child on the grass next to the road. The blistering noonday sun beat down on them without mercy.

The man held up a cardboard sign which read, 'Will Work for Food.' The woman stood next to him. She just stared at the cars that stopped at the red light. The child, probably about two years old, sat on the grass holding a one-armed doll. I noticed all this in the thirty seconds it took for the traffic light to change to green.

I wanted so desperately to give them a few dollars, but if I did that, there wouldn't be enough left to buy the milk and bread. Four dollars will only go so far. As the light changed, I took one last glance at the three of them and sped off feeling both guilty (for not helping them) and sad (because I didn't have enough money to share with them).

As I kept driving, I couldn't get the picture of the three of them out of my mind. The sad, haunting eyes of the young man and his family stayed with me for about a mile. I could take it no longer. I felt their pain and had to do something about it. I turned around and drove back to where I had last seen them.

I pulled up close to them and handed the man two of my four dollars. There were tears in his eyes as he thanked me. I smiled and drove on to the supermarket. Perhaps both milk and bread would be on sale, I thought. And what if I only got milk alone, or just the bread? Well, it would have to do.

I pulled into the parking lot, still thinking about the whole incident, yet feeling good about what I had done. As I stepped out of the car, my foot slid on something on the pavement. There by my feet was a twenty-dollar bill. I just couldn't believe it. I looked all around, picked it up with awe, went into the store and purchased not only bread and milk, but several other items I desperately needed.

I never forgot that incident. It reminded me that the universe was strange and mysterious. It confirmed my belief that you could never out give the universe. I gave away two dollars and got twenty in return. On my way back from the supermarket, I drove by the hungry family and shared five additional dollars with them.

This incident is only one of many that have occurred in my life.

It seems that the more we give, the more we get. It is, perhaps, one of those universal laws that say, 'If you want to receive, you must first give.'

~ John Harricharan (award-winning author of the bestseller, "When You Can Walk on Water, Take the Boat".)

Ponder this:

Some might say finding the twenty-dollar bill was 'a coincidence' or 'sheer luck'. Far from it. It was really the correct application of the Law of Giving in the particular situation. John was financially stressed at the time, yet he gave away 50% of all the money he had on him. The subtlety to the application of the law is that John selflessly gave to a needy person the very thing he needed most at that moment in his life. Think about it.

The Power of Focus

Arjuna (meaning 'one who is pure and unsullied') was the third of five sons of Queen Kunti. Arjuna had immense liking for the sport of archery. He practised this art with great concentration and perseverance. Soon he became the best archer in his land. His teacher (referred to as Gurudev) was very pleased with Arjuna and showed preference toward him. This caused the two older brothers to display a natural adolescence jealousy towards Arjuna.

One day the older brothers openly criticised Gurudev for the preferential attention he gave to Arjuna, telling him that they were no less skilled in archery than Arjuna. In response to their criticism, their teacher arranged a test to decide the best archer amongst them.

Accordingly, a wooden bird was put on a branch of a distant tree. It was partly hidden by the foliage. A prominent artificial eye was painted on the wooden bird. Gurudev called his three students together and said, 'Look my dear students, a bird is sitting on that far off tree. You have to shoot your arrow through its eye. Are you ready?'

Everyone nodded. First the eldest brother was invited to demonstrate his skill. He stretched his bow-string and was about to release the arrow when Gurudev asked him a question.

'O eldest son of Queen Kunti, may I know what is visible to you at this point of time?'

The eldest son replied innocently, 'Why, O Gurudev, I am seeing you, the tree, people around me, and the bird!'

Gurudev said, 'Take aim and shoot'.

The eldest son took aim, held his bow steady, and shot – and completely missed the bird.

Gurudev then invited the second son to demonstrate his skill. Like his elder brother he stretched his bow-string and was about to release the arrow when Gurudev asked him a question.

'O second son of Queen Kunti, may I know what is visible to you at this point of time?'

Sensing that Gurudev was seeking a response that was directly related to the target, the second son quickly replied, 'O Gurudev, I am seeing the sky, the tree, and the bird!'

Gurudev said, 'Take aim and shoot'.

The second son took aim, held his bow steady, and shot. Like his elder brother, he completely missed the bird.

Then it was Arjuna's turn. He readied himself, his bow and arrow in perfect graceful harmony, when the Guru asked him, 'O Arjuna, will you tell me what is being observed by you?'

And Arjuna replied, 'Sir, at this point of time only the eye of the bird is visible to me.' When asked by Gurudev whether he was able to see the bird, the tree, and people around, Arjuna replied in the negative maintaining that he saw the eye of the bird and only the eye of the bird.

Gurudev said, 'Take aim and shoot'.

Arjuna stretched his bow-string, took aim, and shot... and hit the bird in the centre of the eye!

Gurudev said, 'Well done, Arjuna'.

He then explained to the others how Arjuna's immense focus and concentration, and correct approach towards the art of archery gave him the winning edge, and it was for that reason that he regarded Arjuna as his best student.

~ Mahabharatha

Ponder this:

Focus all your attention on what you do want, and get fired up (emotional) about it. In contrast, if you constantly think about what you don't want, you will cause it to manifest: 'What you resist, persists!'

The Crab Bucket

One day a man was walking along the beach when he came upon a fisherman with a bait bucket beside him. He noticed that bucket contained live crabs, but was uncovered. When he asked the fisherman why he did not cover the bucket to prevent the crabs from escaping, the fisherman replied, "Crabs have a 'mass-mentality'". If there is just one crab in the bucket, it would surely crawl out very quickly. However, when there are many crabs in the bucket and one tries to crawl up the side, the others grab hold of it and pull it back down so that it will share the same fate as the rest of them.'

Adapted from various versions on the internet.

Ponder this:

This sort of attack is not uncommon. Humans practise it all the time. If one person tries to do something different, improve oneself, escape an unfavourable environment, or pursue a big dream, some people will try to drag that person back down to share their fate. Every dream you share has the potential to cause jealousy, which is a negative emotion directed toward you. Pursuing your dreams is a courageous act that speaks volumes about you as a person.

We Are All Connected

An interesting experiment that illustrates our connectedness to everything else in existence was done in 1993 under the direction of the United States Army Intelligence and Security Command (INSCOM). Here are the details of that experiment.

White blood cells (leukocytes) were scraped from the mouth of a volunteer, centrifuged, and placed in a test tube. A probe from a recording polygraph (a 'lie' or emotion detector) was inserted in the tube. The donor of the cheek cells was seated in a room separate from his donated cells and shown a television program with many violent scenes. When the volunteer viewed scenes of fighting and killing, the polygraph probe detected extreme excitation in the mouth cells of the donor, despite the test tubes being in a separate room down the hallway. Subsequent repeats of the experiment with the donor and cells separated by up to fifty miles and up to two days after they were donated showed the same results. The donated cells remained energetically, and what scientists call 'non-locally', connected with their donor and seemed to 'remember' where they came from.

(Pearsall, 1999)

Ponder this:

Scientists have confirmed that we are all connected to each other via energy. Science has realised that, on a subatomic level, each of us is influenced by literally everything around us and we, in turn, influence everything else.

Fleas In A Jar

Fleas can jump extremely high. In fact, a flea can jump over 150 times its own height. In an experiment, a scientist placed a number of fleas in a glass jar. They quickly jumped out. He then put the fleas back into the jar and placed a glass lid over the top. The fleas began jumping and hitting the glass lid, falling back down into the jar. After a while, the fleas, conditioned to the presence of the glass lid, began jumping slightly below the glass lid so as not to hit it.

Basically, they got smart. They realised that there was no point knocking their heads against the lid. In fact, they got too smart for their own good. They became conditioned to jump a 'safe' height. When the lid was removed, the fleas continued to jump at a 'safe' height. Essentially, they accepted the limit imposed on them and thereby imposed it on themselves. They were conditioned to remain trapped in the jar forever!

Adapted from various versions on the internet.

Ponder this:

Some beliefs literally put a lid on our potential.

Great Value in Disaster

Thomas Edison's laboratory was virtually destroyed by fire in December, 1914. Although the damage exceeded $2 million, the buildings were only insured for $238 000 because they were made of concrete and thought to be fireproof.

Much of Edison's life's work went up in spectacular flames. Edison's 24-year old son, Charles, frantically searched for his father and finally found him, calmly watching the scene, his face glowing in the reflection, his white hair blowing in the wind.

'My heart ached for him,' said Charles.

'He was 67 — no longer a young man — and everything was going up in flames. When he saw me, he shouted, "Charles, where's your mother?"'

When I told him I didn't know, he said, 'Find her. Bring her here. She will never see anything like this as long as she lives.'

The next morning, Edison looked at the ruins and said, 'There is great value in disaster. All our mistakes are burned up. Thank God we can start anew.'

Three weeks after the fire, Edison managed to deliver his first phonograph.

Adapted from various versions on the internet.

Ponder this:

Surveys, studies and research consistently reaffirm that 85% of success in life depends on attitude, 15% on aptitude. Changing attitudes is something we will always have to do to improve our circumstances in life.

Black Boots

Shelley received a gift that she desperately needed in a very unusual way. She was sitting at Notre Dame in Paris resting her sore feet. She had not brought a comfortable pair of shoes from the States, and her limited budget wouldn't allow her to buy another pair although her feet ached terribly.

Suddenly she felt prompted to walk out of the church and turn left. Following her inner promptings, she made several more turns to arrive at a square. To her surprise she saw a pair of brand new black boots with no signs of wear in exactly her size on top of a trash can. She knew the situation was perfect and had been arranged specifically for her. If the boots had been inside the trash can, she wouldn't have pulled them out. If they had been worn before, she wouldn't have put them on. They were also so stylish that she could never have afforded them herself!

Would this be a story of intuition or synchronicity? Intuition appeared to have led her to the boots. Synchronicity provided her with precisely what she needed. The Universe virtually handed her the boots.

(Lundstrom, 1996)

Ponder this:

If it feels right, follow your intuition. You never know where it might lead. When you are attuned to receiving the seeds of opportunity, even if it is based on a 'gut feeling', the Universe will guide you to the right place at the right time.

Growing Good Corn

There was a Nebraska farmer who grew award-winning corn. Each year he entered his corn in the state fair where it won a blue ribbon. One year a newspaper reporter interviewed him and learned that the farmer shared his seed corn with his neighbours.

'How can you afford to share your best seed corn with your neighbours when they are entering corn in competition with yours each year?' the reporter asked.

'Why sir,' said the farmer, 'didn't you know? The wind picks up pollen from the ripening corn and swirls it from field to field. If my neighbours grow inferior corn, cross-pollination will steadily degrade the quality of my corn. If I am to grow good corn, I must help my neighbours grow good corn.'

He was very much aware of the connectedness of life. His corn could not improve unless his neighbour's corn also improved.

The same is true in other aspects of life. Those who choose to be at peace must help their neighbours to be at peace. Those who choose to live well must help others to live well, for the value of a life is measured by the lives it touches. And those who choose to be happy must help others to find happiness for the welfare of each is bound up with the welfare of all.

The lesson for each of us is this: if we are to prosper, we must help others prosper.

Adapted from various versions on the internet.

Ponder this:

Successful people are dedicated to creating value for others. They understand that their rewards in life are in direct proportion to the services they render to others. Generally, the most successful people are those who have helped the largest number of other people get what they want. Sustainable success is not survival of the fittest; it is about survival of the most cooperative, and it's the most fun!

The Vasily Alexeev Story

Vasily Alexeev, a Soviet weight lifting champion of the 1970s, was the first to break the weight lifting barrier of 500 pounds. However, before this breakthrough, Alexeev was stuck on 499 pounds which he believed was the maximum he could ever lift. Alexeev's trainers changed his limiting belief by misleading him. They put 501.5 pounds on his bar and rigged it so it looked like the 499 pounds, and he lifted it comfortably. He had created a new reality. Soon thereafter other weight lifters went on to break his record because they now knew it was possible to lift more than 500 pounds.

Adapted from various versions on the internet.

Ponder this:

Oftentimes, our limits are only in the mind.

The Power of an Emotive Affirmation

Every human thought, word or deed is a cause that sets off a wave of energy throughout the universe, resulting in desirable or undesirable effects. If there are undesirable effects, it simply means that at some time in the past, there was a thought, word or deed that caused a wave of undesirable energy. As normal, fully-functioning people we are quite literally responsible for everything in our lives. The following excerpt illustrates this concept.

This is the suggestion a man gave to his subconscious mind over a period of about two years: "I would give my right arm to see my daughter cured." It appeared that his daughter had a crippling form of arthritis together with a so-called incurable form of skin disease. Medical treatment had failed to alleviate the condition, and the father had an intense longing for his daughter's healing, and expressed his desire in the words just quoted.

One day the family was out for a drive. Their car was involved in a head-on collision. The father's right arm was torn off at the shoulder. When he came home from the hospital, he discovered that his daughter's arthritis and skin condition had vanished.

(Murphy, 2001)

Ponder this:

Every human thought, word or deed is a *cause* that sets off a wave of energy throughout the universe, resulting in desirable or undesirable *effects*. If there are undesirable effects, it simply means that at some time in the past, there was a thought, word or deed that *caused* a wave of undesirable energy.

The Pike Fish Experiment

A pike fish was once put in a tank along with many small minnows. The pike wasted no time eating all the minnows.

The next day, a glass partition was placed into the tank dividing the tank in two. At feeding time, instead of putting the live minnows in with the pike, the minnows were placed on the other side of the partition. The pike could see the minnows but could not get to them. Unable to detect the glass divider, the pike repeatedly bumped its head trying to reach its dinner. After many painful attempts, it eventually stopped trying.

After a few days, the glass partition was removed from the tank allowing the pike to swim freely amongst the minnows. It could now easily eat the minnows, but the strangest thing happened. Even though the pike hadn't eaten in days and the minnows were within easy reach, it did not go after them. The pain of repeated disappointment had exhausted its will. The pike had been conditioned to believe that it could not catch the minnows and died in the midst of a plentiful supply of food.

Adapted from various versions on the internet.

Ponder this:

We humans become conditioned in much the same way as other creatures. If we keep failing, eventually, we just stop trying.

The Thriving Newspaper Stand

A newspaper stand in New York, only fifteen yards away from another stand, rang up four times as many sales as its competitor. How? After every sale the owner said, 'Thank you.' Customers would go out of their way just to be recognised and thanked.

~ Unknown

Ponder this:

Studies show that not only can gratitude be deliberately cultivated, but can increase levels of wellbeing and happiness in those who cultivate it. Gratitude also adds to the bottom line in very real ways.

Lessons from Geese

When you see geese heading south for the winter, they fly in a V formation. Science has discovered why they fly that way. The following exposition is by Dr Robert McNish (a former science teacher).

- Research has revealed that as each bird flaps its wings, it creates an up lift for the bird immediately behind it. By flying in a V formation, the whole flock adds at least 71% greater flying range than if each bird flew on its own. (People who share a common direction and sense of community get where they are going more quickly and easily because they are traveling on one another's thrust.)

- Whenever a goose falls out of formation, it suddenly feels the drag and resistance of trying to go it alone. It quickly gets back into formation to take advantage of the lifting power of the bird immediately in front. (If we have as much sense as a goose, we will stay in formation and with those who are headed the same way we are.)

- When the lead goose gets tired, he rotates back in the V and another goose flies the point. (It pays to take turns doing the hard jobs. As with geese, people are interdependent of each other's skills, capabilities, talents or resources.)

- The geese honk from behind to encourage those up front to keep up their speed. (Likewise, we need to make sure our honking is encouraging, not discouraging. In groups where there is encouragement, production is much greater.)

- Finally, when a goose gets sick or is wounded by gunfire and falls out, two other geese fall out of formation and follow it down to help and protect it. They stay with the incapacitated goose until it is either able to fly again or dies. Only then will they launch out on their own or with another formation to catch up with their group. (If we have the sense of a goose, we will stand by each other in times of need.)

(Widemark, 2009)

Ponder this:

Leverage is a simple concept and certainly one of the most powerful practices for success in life. Regardless of what you do for a living, you can always do better by applying the power of leverage.

The Roger Bannister Story

Until Roger Bannister ran a mile in under four minutes, many believed that it was physically impossible for a human being to run the mile in that timeframe. Scientists have said that the human heart and physique was not meant to take the strain without serious injury to the runner. When Roger Bannister proved this to be false, within a year, 37 other runners broke the four minute barrier, followed by another 300 within three years. Now thousands more have done the same and run even faster times. The mile isn't run in the Olympics or the world championships any more, but its history is still intriguing. The current world record in the mile is 3:43.13, set by Hicham El Guerrouj of Morocco on July 7, 1999, in Rome's Olympic Stadium.

Adapted from various versions on the internet.

Ponder this:

The history of science and industry is full of examples showing how limiting beliefs impede progress, until someone breaks through, and suddenly a host of others follow. But once Bannister pushed past the 4-minute barrier, the rest of the world saw that it was possible, and the previous record that had stood for nine years was broken routinely.

Jim Carrey and the $10 Million Cheque

Comedy movie star Jim Carrey dreamed of being rich and famous. According to *Biography TV Show,* Carrey wrote himself a post-dated cheque for ten million dollars payable on Thanksgiving 1995. The note in the memo read, 'For Acting Services Rendered.' At that time, Carrey barely had ten thousand dollars in his bank account, let alone ten million! But, he had huge aspirations as an actor, expecting to someday earn at least ten million dollars. Of course, the road to mega success was not easy. He had to deal with many seemingly insurmountable challenges, enough to turn the average actor away from showbiz forever, but not Carrey; he was no quitter. He went on to surpass the ten million pay cheque many times, earning twenty million for *The Cable Guy* in 1996, twenty million for *Liar Liar* in 1997, and twenty-five million for *Bruce Almighty* in 2003. He is reported to average more than twenty million per movie! (wiki.answers.com)

Adapted from various versions on the internet.

Ponder this:

Jim Carrey's experience is not unusual. Most high achievers have equally amazing experiences.

The Maserati Story

There was a gentleman who decided that once he achieved a certain level of income in his business he was going to reward himself with a Maserati. From Wheels, a car magazine, he pulled out a full-page picture of a Maserati and stuck it on his wall at home.

At that time in his life he was driving a battered old bomb, and whenever he drove his old car, he imagined he was in his Maserati. He would carefully back the car out of his garage and then look up at the neighbours' homes. He imagined them shifting the curtains and peering at him in his spanking new car. Then he would take off slowly with the windows wound down.

Living his vision, he would pretend to smell the leather upholstery in the car; he would feel the wood-grain finish on the dashboard; the steering wheel would feel the same as that of a sports car and the sound system matched. When he stopped at the traffic lights, he imagined that the drivers of the vehicles on the right and left sides were looking at and admiring his Maserati.

He continued this visualisation until he reached the level of income he desired. He went to the dealership and chose his car, including the particular colour he wanted.

After a few weeks the car arrived at the dealership and the dealership invited him for a 'presentation' to receive the car — this wasn't your everyday car.

When he came to pick the car up, there was a problem.

'This car is not the same colour as the one I ordered,' he told the dealership. 'It's similar, but the car I ordered is a subtle shade different.'

They checked the original paperwork and, sure enough, they had made a mistake. They quickly acknowledged their error, but the customer was not happy and asked: 'What are you going to do about it?'

The officials got together, had a quick chat and came back to him looking very pleased. They said, 'We are sorry for what had happened. This has never happened before, but we're going to do the right thing by you; we are going to give you a significant discount on this car. In fact, so significant, that it'll blow you away.'

Disappointed and despondent, he replied, 'Look, I'm not interested; I don't like the colour of this car.'

The officials were in a dilemma. They had another discussion and again returned looking genuinely pleased with themselves. They said, 'We have a solution. We have a Maserati of your colour choice here in the showroom. However, it's the more expensive sports edition and it is actually a show car that has been fitted with a lot of extras worth thousands of dollars. Regardless, you can have this car at no extra charge.'

'But,' they added, 'as this is a show car, we have taken it out to the shows, so it's chalked up a little mileage. It has less than 1,000 miles on the clock, but it's a new car and it comes with a new car warranty.'

He looked at them, shook his head and said, 'No, I didn't wait all this time for a second-hand car.'

They tried to convince him, 'It's not a second-hand car or for that matter a demonstrator model; it's a new car with a very small mileage.'

As salesmen do, they appealed to him just to have a look before declining their offer. He was not too keen, but eventually they persuaded him to have a look at the car if only to confirm the colour. As soon as the second car entered the room, the customer's jaw dropped. He was speechless — this was exactly what he was dreaming about. He liked what he saw, but hid his enthusiasm from the salesmen.

He walked around, checking for imperfections. The car was immaculate on the outside. He opened the door, got in on the driver's side and inspected the car on the inside, looking for something he could complain about. The car was impeccable! Also, he loved the sports edition and all the extras. He popped his head out of the window and said, 'Look, I'll take this car.'

Everybody was happy. After the presentation he drove his car home.

When he got inside the house, he stopped to examine the Maserati picture on his wall and then it hit him. The car sitting on the driveway was the exact same car in the picture! It was a snapshot of his car taken at a motor show!

~ Unknown

Ponder this:

It seemed like an amazing coincidence, but this was no coincidence. It's the way the Law of Attraction works.

Do Something

A man distraught by all the pain and suffering he saw all around him broke down and banged his fists into the dirt.

His turned his head upward and yelled at his God.

'Look at this mess. Look at all this pain and suffering. Look at all this killing and hate. God, Oh God! WHY DON'T YOU DO SOMETHING?'

And his God spoke to him and said,
'I did. I sent you.'

Adapted from various versions on the internet.

Ponder this:

The starting point is to accept complete responsibility for your current circumstances. Failure to accept responsibility for your life means giving away your personal power — you give away *control* over your life. While you can give away control over your life, *you cannot give away personal responsibility*. You are always responsible, whether you agree or not.

The Mountain Climber

The mountain climber was determined to reach the summit of a high mountain. After much preparation, he began his adventure. Desiring the glory for such an achievement, he went alone, not telling anyone of his plans. He began his final ascent as daylight faded in the western sky. As nightfall approached, he fought the feeling of being overcome by the encroaching darkness.

Only a few yards from the summit, he slipped, falling off a rocky ledge at a frightful speed. During those anguished moments, his life passed before him. Thinking death was imminent, he felt his safety rope begin to tighten around his waist.

Suddenly he found himself suspended in mid-air. In those first desperate moments a spontaneous prayer sprang from his lips, 'God, please help me!' Then unexpectedly a deep voice from heaven responded, 'What would you have me do?' The mountain climber replied that he wanted to be saved. God answered with another question, 'Do you really think I can save you?'

'Of course, my Lord!' the man replied. Then God told him if he wanted to free himself all he had to do was to cut the rope. After long moments of silence, the man responded by tightening the rope around his waist.

The following morning a local mountain rescue team arrived only to find the man dead. He had frozen to death, his hands wrapped firmly around a rope tied to his waist, hanging just two feet above the ground.

Adapted from various versions on the internet.

Ponder this:

Your specific need and circumstances do not move God as much as faith. God is moved by faith, audacious, unashamed faith. Just as a little flame produces little light, little faith produces little results. If you lack faith and still seek a miraculous outcome, you are fooling yourself. It just won't work. When it comes to trusting God, you either have faith or you don't.

Breaking the Sound Barrier

Chuck Yeager was the first man to fly faster than "Mach 1" (700 miles per hour), which is the speed of sound. There were many failed attempts before he broke the sound barrier on October 14, 1947. A British pilot, Geoffrey de Havilland, had died trying. Despite the dangers, the U.S. air force was determined to be the first. They had developed a small, bullet-shaped aircraft, the Bell X-1, to challenge the sound barrier and had been trying to find a man willing to risk the unknown of supersonic flight.

When Chuck Yeager heard of this opportunity he took up the challenge. At the time, no one knew if a fixed-wing aircraft could fly faster than sound, or if a human pilot could survive the experience. More than half of the engineers involved in building and running the X-1 believed that as soon as the sound barrier was broken, the airplane would disintegrate and no pilot would survive. Yeager believed otherwise; it was his personal belief that the heavy vibration of the plane would actually calm down after reaching Mach 1.

A few nights before the scheduled attempt, Chuck and his wife, Glennis went horseback riding. As 'luck' would have it, Chuck Yeager fell of his horse and broke two ribs on his right side. Yeager taped up his ribs and did his best to hide his condition.

On the day of the flight, it became apparent that Yeager's injured right side wouldn't allow him to shut the door of the Bell X-1. He confessed his problem to Jack Ridley, the flight engineer. Ridley sawed off a short piece of broomstick handle so Yeager would be able to use his left hand to get enough leverage to close the hatch on the X-1.

Early on the morning of October 14, Yeager went up in the B-29 bomber (a much larger plane) that carried the X-1. At an altitude of 7,000 feet, he climbed down a ladder from the B-29 into the little cockpit of the X-1 and locked himself in. The B-29 released the X-1 at 20,000 feet. His jet took off climbing to 40,000 feet, headed for Mach 1 speed. No man had done that before. Yeager wanted to be the first.

At .87 Mach the violent vibrations began, but Yeager continued to push the aircraft faster. Just as he had predicted, at .96 Mach the aircraft steadied and he passed Mach 1. At that moment a giant roar was heard on the desert at the experimental test site — the first man-made sonic boom. Yeager reached Mach 1.05 and stayed above Mach 1 for seven minutes. On his way back to the field he performed victory rolls and wing-over-wing stunts. Yeager broke the sound barrier and etched his name in the history books forever!

Adapted from various versions on the internet.

Ponder this:

When you ask for a big outcome, the Universe will test your willingness to do whatever it takes.

Pray With Gratitude

In his book, Secrets of the Lost Mode of Prayer, bestselling author Gregg Braden shares a wonderful story about a Native American friend, David, who took him on a quest to bring rain during a long drought in New Mexico in the 1990s. Here is that story:

The pair had walked quite a distance to a sacred place used by David's ancestors for prayer and ritual. David took off his shoes and stepped into the circle. He acknowledged the four directions and his ancestors, placed his hands in prayer position, closed his eyes and then stood motionless in silence.

After a few moments, he said he had finished and was ready to leave.

Gregg, who was waiting for something more elaborate to happen, said, I thought you were going to pray for rain.

'No,' he replied. 'I said that I would pray rain. If I had prayed for rain, it could never happen.'

When Gregg asked him why, he said 'It's because the moment you pray for something to occur, you've just acknowledged that it's not existing in that moment — and you may actually be denying the very thing you'd like to bring forward in your prayers.'

He described how the elders of his village had shared the secrets of prayer with him when he was young boy. The key, he said, is that when we ask for something to happen, we give power to what we do not have.

'If you pray for rain, you affirm the lack of what you want and you, therefore, create more lack of what you want – in this case, rain. When you pray rain [instead of pray for rain], you affirm the existence of rain right now, right here, in this moment. You offer gratitude for what you already have or expect to have,' he explained.

'Well, if you didn't pray for rain just now when you closed your eyes, what did you do?' asked Gregg.

He said, 'When I closed my eyes, I felt the feeling of what it feels like after there's been so much rain that I can stand with my naked feet in the mud of my pueblo village. I smelled the smells of rainwater rolling off the earthen walls of our homes. And I felt what it feels like to walk through a field of corn that is chest high because of all the rain that has fallen. In that way, I plant a seed for the possibility of that rain, and then I give thanks of gratitude and appreciation.'

'You mean gratitude for the rain that you've created?' asked Gregg.

And he said, 'No, we don't create the rain. I'm giving thanks of gratitude and appreciation for the opportunity to commune with the forces of creation.'

As the story goes, it did indeed rain thereafter.

(Braden, 2006)

Ponder this:

According to Gregg Braden, the lost mode of prayer is a prayer that's based solely in *feeling*. So, don't complain that your prayers don't work. Instead, change how you pray. Stop asking for what you want and need, and start praying to God with gratitude for prayers answered.

The Parable of the Butterfly

A man found a cocoon of a butterfly and he watched the butterfly for several hours as it struggled to force its body through that little hole. Then it seemed to stop making any progress. It appeared as if it had gotten as far as it could and it could go no further.

So the man decided to help the butterfly. He took a pair of scissors and snipped off the remaining bit of the cocoon. The butterfly then emerged easily. But it had a swollen body and small, shriveled wings.

The man continued to observe the butterfly, expecting that, at any moment, the butterfly would stretch its wings and take flight. That did not happen.

The wings had not grown enough, and the butterfly spent the rest of its life crawling around with a swollen body and shriveled wings. It never was able to fly.

Adapted from various versions on the internet.

Ponder this:

The man, in his kindness and haste, did not understand that before a butterfly can emerge out of its cocoon, it has to go through a struggle. Each time it lunges to break out of its cocoon, acids are removed from its wings. In prematurely breaking open the cocoon, the butterfly could die from those acids.

We cannot escape the challenges that life dishes out to us as we move towards our goals. They are there to teach us important lessons and strengthen us in some way. To make progress, we must face life's challenges and overcome them. Trying to short circuit the learning process can have harmful consequences.

The Remarkable Soichiro Honda

Like most other countries, Japan was hit badly by the Great Depression of the 1930s. At this time Soichiro Honda was an expert auto mechanic with his own workshop in the city of Hahamatsu. In 1938, Soichiro Honda started a little factory to manufacture piston rings for motor car engines.

His intention was to sell the piston rings to Toyota. He labored night and day, even slept in the workshop, always believing he could perfect his design and develop a quality product. Desperate for funds, he pawned his wife's jewelry to finance his business.

Finally, the day came when he completed his piston ring and was able to take a working sample to Toyota. Toyota rejected his creation, saying that the rings did not meet their standards. Soichiro suffered ridicule when the engineers laughed at his design.

He refused to give up. Rather than focus on his failure, he continued working towards his goal. He went back to school to study metallurgy and learn how to work with metal. After two more years of struggle and a redesign of his product, he finally won a contract with Toyota in 1940.

However, at this time, the Japanese government was gearing up for war. With the contract in hand, Soichiro Honda needed to build a factory to supply Toyota, but building materials were in short supply. Still he would not quit! He invented a new concrete-making process that enabled him to build the factory.

With the factory now built, he was ready for production, but the factory was bombed twice. Also, steel became unavailable. Was this the end of the road for Honda? No!

He started collecting surplus gasoline cans discarded by US fighters. 'Gifts from President Truman,' he called them, and they became the new raw material for his rebuilt manufacturing process. Finally, an earthquake destroyed the factory.

After the war, an extreme gasoline shortage forced people to walk or use bicycles. Riding his bicycle to work was too slow, so Soichiro built a tiny engine and attached it to his bicycle. People in his neighbourhood were impressed and wanted one, too. Unfortunately, raw materials to build the engines were in short supply and he was unable to meet the demand.

Unwilling to accept defeat, Soichiro Honda wrote to 18 000 bicycle store owners and, in an inspiring letter, asked them to help him revitalize Japan. Approximately 5000 responded and supported his quest to build his small bicycle engines. Unfortunately, the first models were too bulky to work well, so he continued to develop and adapt. Finally, the small engine named 'The Super Cub' became a reality and was an outstanding success. Having achieved success in Japan, Honda then began exporting his Super Cub motorcycles to Europe and America.

The story does not end there. In the 1970s there was another gas shortage and automotive trend shifted to small cars. Honda was quick to pick up on the trend. Expert in small engine design, his company started making small cars, smaller than anyone had seen before, and rode another wave of success.

Today, Honda Corporation is one of the world's largest automobile companies. Honda succeeded because one man made a truly committed decision, acted upon it, and made adjustments on a continuous basis. Failure was not an option for Soichiro Honda.

Adapted from various versions on the internet.

Ponder this:

Everyone knows how to thrive in the good times. It is the trying times that separate those of true substance from those who portray an image of substance, that is, those who really walk the talk from those who merely talk. The hard times prepare us for greater accomplishments in life. It is through trials and tribulations that the human spirit triumphs over itself.

Two Frogs in Trouble

One day, on a farm, a group of frogs were hopping along together when suddenly — oops! — two of them, Big Frog and Little Frog, had the misfortune to jump straight into a bucket of fresh milk. They began frantically paddling in an attempt to escape, but they were no match for the tall slippery sides of the bucket. There was no place to rest. Death seemed certain.

Outside, near the edge of the pail, many of their mates watched as they struggled in vain to get out. Feeling content that they were not in such a predicament, their mates jeered from the outside, saying such things as:

'Give up. Don't waste your time. Accept your fate.'

'It's hopeless. It's only a matter of time before you drown.'

'Why struggle against the inevitable; you are going to die?'

Hours passed as the pair continued to paddle for dear life. As poor old Big Frog became exhausted, his swimming became slower and slower and he felt inclined to give up. Speaking softly, he said, 'I am too tired to keep swimming. What's the point of going on; we are going to die anyway.' Sensing that Big Frog had lost hope, Little Frog, in his screechy little voice, shouted, 'Please keep paddling; I know you can do it. To give up is to die!'

Unfortunately all the jeering from their mates got the better of Big Frog and he gave up and stopped swimming, and slowly sunk to the bottom of the bucket and drowned. Little Frog, filled with grief and fear, just kept on paddling. The longer he paddled, the more tired he became. He could see his mates on the outside gesturing and shouting. And, the more they gestured and shouted, the harder he paddled. They continued to jeer and laugh at him, and he just kept on keeping on.

As he paddled, the milk became thicker and thicker making it even harder for him to keep afloat. But, he was no quitter; he simply increased his effort. Two more hours passed and the tiny legs of the determined little frog were almost paralysed with exhaustion. It seemed as if he would not be able to keep the paddling up for much longer. But, then he thought of Big Frog and said to himself, 'Well, to give up is to be dead, so I will keep on swimming until I die – if death is to come – but I'll not cease trying. While there is life, there is hope'.

Intoxicated with determination, Little Frog kept on paddling around and around the pail, chopping the milk into white waves. After a while, just as he felt numb and thought he was going to drown, he suddenly felt something solid beneath him. To his amazement, he found that he was resting on a lump of butter which he had churned by his incessant paddling! And, so Little Frog leaped out of the milk pail to freedom.

Clearly, Little Frog was very different from Big Frog who had drowned in the milk bucket. You would probably say that Little Frog was not a quitter; he was a survivor; he was persistent; he had heart; and so on. You would be right on all counts.

However, there was another, more significant difference between Little Frog and Big Frog. Little Frog was deaf. He couldn't hear his mates jeering and discouraging him. He thought that they were cheering and encouraging him. He thought they were saying such things as:

'Keep going, Little Frog. You can do it.'

'Don't give up.'

'We are all with you. Give it your best shot.'

'Go for it, Little Frog. Go for it!'

Adapted from various versions on the internet.

Ponder this:

If you persist, you will succeed.

Edmund Hillary - Scaling Mount Everest

New Zealand adventurer, Edmund Hillary and Nepalese sherpa, Tenzing Norgay made history at 11:30 a.m. on May 29, 1953. They climbed to the top of Mount Everest, the highest point on Earth, approximately 8882 metres above sea level. Being the first to set foot atop Mount Everest, the accomplishment brought Hillary worldwide fame and he was knighted that same year, becoming Sir Edmund Hillary. He was an overnight celebrity. However, Hillary's success did not come easily. He had to grow into the success he had become.

Since 1922, several attempts to challenge Everest had failed before it was finally conquered in 1953. In 1951, Hillary was part of the British Reconnaissance expedition to Everest. However, this expedition was unsuccessful. In 1952, Hillary was back in the Himalayas as part of an expedition that attempted to climb the Cho Oyu, which is part of the Himalayan range, about 30 km west of Everest. This expedition also failed due to the lack of a route on the Nepal side.

Several weeks after this failed attempt, Hillary was asked to address a group in England. Hillary walked on stage to a thunderous applause. The audience was recognizing an attempt at greatness, but Edmund Hillary saw himself as undeserving. He had not completed what he had set out to do. No one had conquered the mountain, yet.

At some point during his speech, Hillary moved away from the microphone and walked to the edge of the platform. He made a fist and pointed it at a picture of Mount Everest, which hung on the wall. He said, 'Mount Everest, you beat me the first time, but I'll beat you the next time because you've grown all you are going to grow and I'm still growing.'

Adapted from various versions on the internet.

Ponder this:

History bears testimony that this statement to the picture of Mount Everest was not made lightly. Edmund Hillary was resolute. A year later, he became the first person to conquer Mount Everest, the tallest mountain in the world!

Elephant and the Blind Man

Once upon a time, there lived six blind men in a village. One day the villagers told them, "Hey, there is an elephant in the village today."

They had no idea what an elephant was. They decided, "Even though we will not be able to see it, let us go and feel it anyway." All of them went where the elephant was. Every one of them touched the elephant.

"Hey, the elephant is like a pillar," said the first man who touched the leg.

"Oh, no! it is like a rope," said the second man who touched the tail.

"Oh, no! it is like a thick branch of a tree," said the third man who touched the trunk of the elephant.

"It is like a big hand fan" said the fourth man who touched the ear of the elephant.

"It is like a huge wall," said the fifth man who touched the belly of the elephant.

"It is like a solid pipe," said the sixth man who touched the tusk of the elephant.

They began to argue about the elephant and every one of them insisted that he was right. It looked like they were getting agitated. A wise man was passing by and he saw this. He stopped and asked them, "What is the matter?" They said, "We cannot agree to what the elephant is like." Each one of them told what he thought the elephant was like. The wise man calmly explained to them, "All of you are right. The reason every one of you is describing it differently is because each one of you touched a different part of the elephant. So, actually the elephant has all those features as each of you described."

"Oh!" everyone said. There was no more fight. They felt happy that they were all right.

~ Anonymous

Ponder this:

The "truth" an individual sees in a situation, depends on his/her 'perspective'. One person's perspective may not align with another's. Therefore, understand that people have their "own" truth. Acceptance of this difference can prevent arguments.

A Tale of Two Shoe Salesmen

There is a tale about these two shoe salesmen who travel to a third world country in search of new business opportunities.

One man calls his wife the moment he lands, telling her, "Honey, I'm coming back home. There's no hope here. Nobody here is wearing shoes, so there's no one to sell to." He boards the next flight home.

The second man calls his wife and says, "Honey, you wouldn't believe what I found here. There is so much opportunity. No one here is wearing shoes. I can sell to the whole country!"

~ Unknown

Ponder this:

There's opportunity everywhere. When we have a positive mental attitude, amazing things begin to happen. We "accidently" bump into the right people; we move in the right circles; we 'find' the right solutions. It all starts with "opening" the mind to new possibilities.

Attitude is Everything

Jerry is the kind of guy you love to hate. He is always in a good mood and always has something positive to say. When someone would ask him how he was doing, he would reply, "If I were any better, I would be twins!"

He was a unique manager because he had several waiters who had followed him around from restaurant to restaurant. The reason the waiters followed Jerry was because of his attitude. He was a natural motivator. If an employee was having a bad day, Jerry was there telling the employee how to look on the positive side of the situation.

Seeing this style really made me curious, so one day I went up to Jerry and asked him, I don't get it! You can't be a positive person all of the time. How do you do it?" Jerry replied, "Each morning I wake up and say to myself, Jerry, you have two choices today. You can choose to be in a good mood or you can choose to be in a bad mood. I choose to be in a good mood. Each time something bad happens, I can choose to be a victim or I can choose to learn from it. I choose to learn from it. Every time someone comes to me complaining, I can choose to accept their complaining or I can point out the positive side of life. I choose the positive side of life.

"Yeah, right, it's not that easy," I protested. "Yes it is," Jerry said. "Life is all about choices. When you cut away all the junk, every situation is a choice. You choose how you react to situations. You choose how people will affect your mood.

You choose to be in a good mood or bad mood. The bottom line: It's your choice how you live life."

I reflected on what Jerry said. Soon thereafter, I left the restaurant industry to start my own business. We lost touch, but I often thought about him when I made a choice about life instead of reacting to it. Several years later, I heard that Jerry did something you are never supposed to do in the restaurant business...he left the back door open one morning and was held up at gun point by three armed robbers. While trying to open the safe, his hand, shaking from nervousness, slipped off the combination. The robbers panicked and shot him. Luckily, Jerry was found relatively quickly and rushed to the local trauma center. After 18 hours of surgery and weeks of intensive care, Jerry was released from the hospital with fragments of the bullets still in his body.

I saw Jerry about six months after the accident. When I asked him how he was, he replied, "If I were any better, I'd be twins. Wanna see my scars?" I declined to see his wounds, but did ask him what had gone through his mind as the robbery took place. "The first thing that went through my mind was that I should have locked the back door," Jerry replied. "Then, as I lay on the floor, I remembered that I had two choices: I could choose to live or I could choose to die. I chose to live."

"Weren't you scared? Did you lose consciousness?" I asked. Jerry continued, "...the paramedics were great. They kept telling me I was going to be fine. But when they wheeled me into the ER and I saw the expressions on the faces of the doctors and nurses, I got really scared. In their eyes, I read 'he's a dead man.' I knew I needed to take action." "What did you do?" I asked. "Well, there was a big burly nurse shouting questions at me," said Jerry. "She asked if I was allergic to anything. 'Yes' I replied. The doctors and nurses stopped working as they waited for my reply. I took a deep breath and yelled, 'BULLETS!'

Over their laughter, I told them, 'I am choosing to live. Operate on me as if I am alive, not dead'." Jerry lived thanks to the skill of his doctors, but also because of his amazing attitude. I learned from him that every day we have the choice to live fully.

Attitude, after all, is everything.

~ Francie Baltazar-Schwartz

Ponder this:

Our attitude towards life determines life's attitude towards us. Realise that whatever your attitude, be it positive or negative, that's the response you'll receive in return from those around you.

The Proud Red Rose

One beautiful spring day a red rose blossomed in a forest. Many kinds of trees and plants grew there. As the rose looked around, a pine tree nearby said, "What a beautiful flower. I wish I was that lovely." Another tree said, "Dear pine, do not be sad, we can't have everything."

The rose turned its head and remarked, "It seems that I am the most beautiful plant in this forest."

A sunflower raised its yellow head and asked, "Why do you say that? In this forest there are many beautiful plants. You are just one of them."

The red rose replied, "I see everyone looking at me and admiring me." Then the rose looked at a cactus and said, "Look at that ugly plant full of thorns!"

The pine tree said, "Red rose, what kind of talk is this? Who can say what beauty is? You have thorns too."

The proud red rose looked angrily at the pine and said, "I thought you had good taste! You do not know what beauty is at all. You can't compare my thorns to that of the cactus."

"What a proud flower", thought the trees.

The rose tried to move its roots away from the cactus, but it could not move. As the days passed, the red rose would look at the cactus and say insulting things, like: This plant is useless? How sorry I am to be his neighbor."

The cactus never got upset and he even tried to advise the rose, saying, "God did not create any form of life without a purpose."

Spring passed, and the weather became very warm. Life became difficult in the forest, as the plants and animals needed water and no rain fell. The red rose began to wilt. One day the rose saw sparrows stick their beaks into the cactus and then fly away, refreshed.

This was puzzling, and the red rose asked the pine tree what the birds were doing. The pine tree explained that the birds got water from the cactus.

"Does it not hurt when they make holes?" asked the rose.

"Yes, but the cactus does not like to see any birds suffer," replied the pine.

The rose opened its eyes in wonder and said, "The cactus has water?"

"Yes you can also drink from it. The sparrow can bring water to you if you ask the cactus for help."

The rose felt too ashamed of its insulting behavior toward the cactus to ask for water. Finally, when the rose became desperate, it did ask the cactus for help. The cactus kindly agreed and the birds filled their beaks with water and watered the rose's roots.

Adapted from various versions on the internet.

Ponder this:

Never judge anyone by their appearance.

The Tale of the Sands

A stream, from its source in far-off mountains, passing through every kind of description of countryside, at last reached the sands of the desert. Just as it had crossed every other barrier, the stream expected to cross this one, but it found that as fast as it flowed into the desert, just as fast its waters disappeared into the sands.

It was convinced, however, that its destiny was to cross this desert and make its way to the sea, and yet there was no way.

Before long, the stream heard a voice whispering from the desert itself, 'The wind crosses the desert, so can the stream'.

'Yes, but the wind can fly!' cried out the stream, as it kept dashing itself into the desert sands.

'You'll never get across that way,' the desert whispered once again. 'You'll have to let the wind carry you.'

'But how?' cried out the stream.

'You have to let the wind absorb you.'

This idea was not acceptable to the stream. After all, it had never been absorbed before. It didn't want to lose its identity. So, it asked the desert:

'Once I give myself to the winds, how can I be sure of ever becoming a stream again?'

'The wind,' said the desert, 'performs this function. It takes up water, carries it over the desert, and then lets it fall again. Falling as rain, the water again becomes a river.'

The desert told the stream that, if it wished, it could continue to flow into the sand, and that one day, after many, many years, it might even become a swamp or mud puddle on the desert's edge. But, it would never cross the desert as long as it remained a stream.

'Why can't I remain the same stream that I am?' asked the stream.

'You cannot remain as you are. Either you give yourself to the wind or you become a swamp,' the desert said. 'By giving yourself to the wind, your essential part is carried away and forms a stream again. You are called what you are even today because you do not know which part of you is the essential one.'

The stream could not believe it, but realised that the best that could be attained without attempting the suggestion would be to become a swamp. Either way the stream could not stay as it was.

The stream was silent for a long time, listening to certain echoes deep within itself, remembering parts of itself having been held in the arms of the wind before. And then slowly, the stream surrendered to the heat of the sun, raised its vapors into the welcoming arms of the wind and was borne upward and over the desert in great white clouds.

As it passed beyond the mountains on the desert's far side, there it began to fall as a gentle rain.

At first it was hushed and quiet, trickling down the rocky slopes. But gradually it increased in strength, as rivulets ran over the rocks and around the bent and twisted trees that grew there. And soon it was flowing as swift currents of water into the beginning of a stream, continuing its journey to the sea.

(Shah, 1969)

Ponder this:

The stream is a metaphor for life. The reality is that you are an ever flowing stream of consciousness subjected to ongoing change. Like the mountain stream, each of us is called upon to change continuously in every arena of our existence, whether it is in our family life, in our profession or in the world at large.

Change happens to us whether we like it or not, and whether we are prepared for it or not. Not seeing the need for change is one thing, but seeing it, yet still resisting, can be the difference between being a stagnant mud puddle and a free flowing spirit heading towards its destiny. Embrace change and use it to transform your life.

The Burnt Biscuit

When I was a kid, every now and then, my mom liked to make breakfast food for dinner. I remember one night in particular when she had made breakfast after a long, hard day at work.

On that evening so long ago, my mom placed a plate of eggs, a sausage and extremely burned biscuits in front of my dad. I remember waiting to see if anyone noticed! Yet all my dad did was reach for his biscuit, smile at my mom and ask me how my day was at school. I don't remember what I told him that night, but I do remember watching him smear butter and jelly on that biscuit and eat every bite!

When I got up from the table that evening, I remember hearing my mom apologize to my dad for burning the biscuits. And I'll never forget what he said: "Honey, I love burned biscuits."

Later that night, I went to kiss Daddy good night and I asked him if he really liked his biscuits burned. He wrapped me in his arms and said, "Your Momma put in a hard day at work today and she's real tired. And besides, a little burnt biscuit never hurt anyone!"

Adapted from various versions on the internet.

Ponder this:

Remember, no one is perfect and we all make mistakes, more so when we are tired.

Perception

Back in January 2007, commuters hurried by without realizing that the busker playing at the entrance to a metro station in Washington, D.C. was none other than the virtuoso concert violinist Joshua Bell. This was a stunt, an experiment ("In a banal setting at an inconvenient time, would beauty transcend?") concocted by *The Washington Post* columnist Gene Weingarten and which later won a Pulitzer Prize for the story.

During the 40 minutes that Grammy-winning violinist Joshua Bell played, hardly anyone stopped. In fact, out of 1,097 people that passed by Bell, only 27 gave any money, a mere 7 actually stopped and listened for any length of time, and only one person recognised him.

And how much did he make? The violinist who can command thousands for each concert performance on the greatest concert stages in the world made just $52.17, which includes $20 from the one person who *did* recognise him.

Adapted from various versions on the internet.

Ponder this:

The demands and distractions of our fast-paced workaday world can indeed stand in the way of appreciating truth and beauty and other contemplative delights when we encounter them.

Don't Sell Yourself Short

The human race is a story of people selling themselves short and settling for less than they are capable of achieving. Instead of *achievement,* we get addicted to *activity*. In time we confuse activity with achievement.

The following story is a good analogy of how many of us live our lives.

The renowned French Naturalist, Jean-Henri Fabre, conducted an interesting experiment with processionary caterpillars, so-called because of their habit of following a lead caterpillar, each with its eyes half closed and head fitted snugly against the rear end of the preceding caterpillar.

Fabre was able to get them on to the rim of a large flowerpot with the lead caterpillar connected up to the last one, thus forming a complete circle, which started moving around in a procession, with neither beginning nor end. In the middle of the circle created by their procession, he placed some pine needles, their favourite food. Each caterpillar followed the one ahead thinking that it was heading for the food.

The naturalist expected that after a while they would discover their predicament or get tired of their useless procession, and move off in some new direction. But that was not the case. Through sheer force of habit, the creeping circle of caterpillars kept moving around the rim of the pot, quite oblivious to the world around them. They were busy being busy, blindly following the caterpillar in front.

went for seven days and nights! less activity, the caterpillars started exhaustion and starvation. They vere searching for just inches away. nd this circular arrangement, they pillar in front was leading.

llars were locked into this lifestyle instincts, habits, past experience, ecedent — the way they always *y, they got nowhere.*

Adapted from various versions on the internet.

Ponder this:

The caterpillars confused activity with accomplishment. They confused *being busy* with *results*. Many of us are guilty of the same mistake, but we have no excuse because we are blessed with intelligence and freewill, and therefore the ability to change our direction anytime we choose. However, we are creatures of habit and can all too readily get into ruts, which can become vicious circles, and which, in turn, lead nowhere except to a life of frustration and dysfunction, if not mediocrity.

Three Red Marbles

I was at the corner grocery store buying some early potatoes and noticed a small boy, delicate of bone and feature, ragged but clean, hungrily apprising a basket of freshly picked green peas.

I paid for my potatoes but was also drawn to the display of fresh green peas. I am a pushover for creamed peas and new potatoes.

Pondering the peas, I couldn't help overhearing the conversation between Mr. Miller (the store owner) and the ragged boy next to me.

"Hello Barry, how are you today?"

"H'lo, Mr. Miller. Fine, thank ya. Jus' admirin' them peas. They sure look good."

"They are good, Barry. How's your Ma?"

"Fine. Gittin' stronger alla' time."

"Good. Anything I can help you with?"

"No, Sir. Jus' admirin' them peas."

"Would you like to take some home?" asked Mr. Miller.

"No, Sir. Got nuthin' to pay for 'em with."

"Well, what have you to trade me for some of those peas?"

"All I got's my prize marble here."

"Is that right? Let me see it" said Miller.

"Here 'tis. She's a dandy."

"I can see that. Hmmmmm, only thing is this one is blue and I sort of go for red. Do you have a red one like this at home?" the store owner asked.

"Not zackley but almost."

"Tell you what. Take this sack of peas home with you and next trip this way let me look at that red marble". Mr. Miller told the boy.

"Sure will. Thanks Mr. Miller." Mrs. Miller, who had been standing nearby, came over to help me. With a smile she said, "There are two other boys like him in our community, all three are in very poor circumstances. Jim just loves to bargain with them for peas, apples, tomatoes, or whatever. When they come back with their red marbles, and they always do, he decides he doesn't like red after all and he sends them home with a bag of produce for a green marble or an orange one, when they come on their next trip to the store."

I left the store smiling to myself, impressed with this man. A short time later I moved to Colorado, but I never forgot the story of this man, the boys, and their bartering for marbles.

Several years went by, each more rapid than the previous one. Just recently I had occasion to visit some old friends in that Idaho community and while I was there learned that Mr. Miller had died. They were having his visitation that evening and knowing my friends wanted to go, I agreed to accompany them. Upon arrival at the mortuary we fell into line to meet the relatives of the deceased and to offer whatever words of comfort we could.

Ahead of us in line were three young men. One was in an army uniform and the other two wore nice haircuts, dark suits and white shirts... all very professional looking. They approached Mrs. Miller, standing composed and smiling by her husband's casket. Each of the young men hugged her, kissed her on the cheek, spoke briefly with her and moved on to the casket.

Her misty light blue eyes followed them as, one by one, each young man stopped briefly and placed his own warm hand over the cold pale hand in the casket. Each left the mortuary awkwardly, wiping his eyes.

Our turn came to meet Mrs. Miller. I told her who I was and reminded her of the story from those many years ago and what she had told me about her husband's bartering for marbles. With her eyes glistening, she took my hand and led me to the casket.

"Those three young men who just left were the boys I told you about. They just told me how they appreciated the things Jim "traded" them. Now, at last, when Jim could not change his mind about color or size... they came to pay their debt."

"We've never had a great deal of the wealth of this world," she confided, "but right now, Jim would consider himself the richest man in Idaho."

With loving gentleness she lifted the lifeless fingers of her deceased husband.

Resting underneath were three exquisitely shined red marbles.

We will not be remembered by our words, but by our kind deeds.

~ W.E Peterson

Ponder this:

Life is not measured by the number of breaths we take, but by the moments that take our breath away.

Dick Hoyt – "Father of the Century"

Eighty-five times Dick Hoyt pushed his disabled son, Rick, 26.2 miles in marathons. Eight times he's not only pushed him 26.2 miles in a wheelchair but also towed him 2.4 miles in a dinghy while swimming and pedaled him 112 miles in a seat on the handlebars-all in the same day.

Dick's also pulled him cross-country skiing, taken him on his back mountain climbing and once hauled him across the U.S. on a bike. Makes taking your son and daughter bowling look a little lame, right?

And what has Rick done for his father? Not much – except save his life. This love story began in Winchester, Massachusetts, 43 years ago when Rick was strangled by the umbilical cord during birth, leaving him brain-damaged and unable to control his limbs. "He'll be a vegetable the rest of his life", Dick says doctors told him and his wife Judy. And, when Rick was nine months old; "Put him in an institution".

But the Hoyt's weren't buying it. They noticed the way Rick's eyes followed them around the room. When Rick was 11 they took him to the engineering department at Tufts University and asked if there was anything to help them and their boy communicate. "No way," Dick says he was told, "There's nothing going on in his brain".

"Tell him a joke", Dick countered. They did. Rick laughed. Turns out a lot was going on in his brain.

Rigged up with a computer that allowed him to control the cursor by touching a switch with the side of his head, Rick was finally able to communicate. First words? "Go Bruins!"

After a high school classmate was paralyzed in an accident and the school organized a charity run for him, Rick pecked out, "Dad, I want to do that". Yeah, right. How was Dick, a self-described "porker" who never ran more than a mile at a time, going to push his son five miles? Still, he tried. "Then it was me who was handicapped", Dick says. "I was sore for two weeks".

That day changed Rick's life. "Dad", he typed, "when we were running, it felt like I wasn't disabled anymore!"

And that sentence changed Dick's life. He became obsessed with giving Rick that feeling as often as he could. He got into such hard-belly shape that he and Rick were ready to try the 1979 Boston Marathon.

"No way," Dick was told by a race official. The Hoyt's weren't quite a single runner, and they weren't quite a wheelchair competitor.

For a few years Dick and Rick just joined the massive field and ran anyway, then they found a way to get into the race officially. In 1983 they ran a marathon so fast they made the qualifying time for Boston the following year.

Then somebody said, "Hey, Dick, why not a triathlon?" How's a guy who never learned to swim and hadn't ridden a bike since he was six going to haul his 110-pound kid through a triathlon? Still, Dick tried. Now they've done 212 triathlons, including four grueling 15-hour Iron man's in Hawaii. It must be a buzzkill to be a 25-year-old stud getting passed by an old guy towing a grown man in a dinghy, don't you think?

"Hey, Dick, why not see how you'd do on your own?"

"No way", he says. Dick does it purely for "the awesome feeling" he gets seeing Rick with a cantaloupe smile as they run, swim and ride together.

This year, at ages 65 and 43, Dick and Rick finished their 24th Boston Marathon in 5083rd place out of more than 20,000 starters. Their best time? Two hours, 40 minutes in 1992 — only 35 minutes off the world record, which, in case you don't keep track of these things, happens to be held by a guy who was not pushing another man in a wheelchair at the time.

"No question about it", Rick types. "My dad is the Father of the Century."

And Dick got something else out of all this too. Two years ago he had a mild heart attack during a race. Doctors found that one of his arteries was 95% clogged. "If you hadn't been in such great shape," one doctor told him, "You probably would've died 15 years ago." So, in a way, Dick and Rick saved each other's life.

Rick, who has his own apartment (he gets home care) and works in Boston, and Dick, retired from the military and living in Holland, Massachusetts always find ways to be together. They give speeches around the country and compete in some backbreaking race every weekend, including this Father's Day.

That night, Rick will buy his dad dinner, but the thing he really wants to give him is a gift he can never buy.

"The thing I'd most like", Rick types, "is that my dad would sit in the chair and I would push him once."

~ Rick Reilly

Ponder this:

We all have untapped potential that can be tapped in the right circumstances if we so choose.

Eyes 'Slant'

A prominent Chinese came to America to be educated in American ways. He attended the University of Chicago.

One day President Harper met this young Oriental on the campus, stopped to chat with him for a few minutes, and asked what had impressed him as being the most noticeable characteristic of the American people.

"Why," the Chinaman exclaimed, "the queer slant of your eyes. Your eyes are off slant!"

What do we say about the Chinese? We refuse to believe that which we do not understand. We foolishly believe that our own limitations are the proper measure of limitations. Sure, the other fellow's eyes are "off slant," BECAUSE THEY ARE NOT THE SAME AS OUR OWN.

(Hill, 2014)

Ponder this:

We all have a view of the world and it is mostly made up of what we have experienced personally through our senses of sight, sound, smell, taste and touch. However, our senses are limited. Therefore, our view of the world is limited. The sooner we acknowledge this, the better.

Challenges Make Us Stronger

If you're breathing, you have difficulties. It's the way of life. And believe it or not, most of your problems may actually be good for you! Let me explain.

Maybe you have seen the Great Barrier Reef, stretching some 1,800 miles from New Guinea to Australia. Tour guides regularly take visitors to view the reef. On one tour, the guide was asked an interesting question. "I notice that the lagoon side of the reef looks pale and lifeless, while the ocean side is vibrant and colourful," a traveller observed. "Why is this?"

The guide gave an interesting answer: "The coral around the lagoon side is in still water, with no challenge for its survival. It dies early. The coral on the ocean side is constantly being tested by wind, waves, and storms — surges of power. It has to fight for survival every day of its life. As it is challenged and tested it changes and adapts. It grows healthy. It grows strong. And it reproduces." Then he added this telling note: "That's the way it is with every living organism."

That's how it is with people. Challenged and tested, we come alive! Like coral pounded by the sea, we grow. Physical demands can cause us to grow stronger. Mental and emotional stress can produce tough-mindedness and resilience. Spiritual testing can produce strength of character and faithfulness.

So, you have problems — no problem! Just tell yourself, "There I grow again!"

~ Unknown

Ponder this:

Like the reef corals that thrive in a high-energy environment, so do people who will not surrender to the challenges of their environment. Essentially, a challenging environment stimulates growth and development.

Looking Up

Back in the days of sailing ships, a young sailor went to sea for the first time. The ship encountered a heavy storm in the North Atlantic. The young sailor was commanded to go aloft and trim the sails. As the young sailor started to climb, he made the mistake of looking down. The roll of the ship combined with the tossing of the waves, made for a frightening experience. The young man started to lose his balance. At that moment, an older sailor underneath him shouted, "Look up, son, look up!" The young sailor looked up and regained his balance.

(Ziglar, 1975)

Ponder this:

When things seem bad, look to see if you are not facing the wrong direction. When the outlook isn't good, try the up-look — it's always good.

Shake It Off and Step Up

One day a farmer's mule fell into a well. The animal cried piteously for hours as the farmer tried to figure out a way to get him out.

The well was deep and the mule was heavy. The farmer certainly did not have the resources to lift the animal out. Finally he decided the mule was too old and the unused well needed to be covered anyway, so he would bury the mule in the well and, in that way, solve two problems at the same time.

He immediately enlisted his neighbors to help him cover up the well and put the mule out of his misery. They all grabbed shovels and began throwing dirt into the well. At first, the mule realized what was happening and became hysterical. Soon, to everyone's amazement, he quieted down. It suddenly dawned upon him that every time a shovel load of dirt landed on him, he should shake it off and step up! So, with every shovel of dirt that hit his back, the mule would shake it off and step up.

Eventually, to everyone's amazement, the old mule, exhausted and dirty, but very much alive, stepped up over the edge of the well and trotted off!

Adapted from various versions on the internet.

Ponder this:

Life is a challenge. From time to time life is going to shovel dirt on you. Stop whinnying like a mule; face the challenge – just shake it off and take a step up... and you too will come out on top!

A Cherokee Parable

An elderly Cherokee Native American was teaching his grandchildren about life.

He said to them, "A fight is going on inside me, it is a terrible fight and it is between two wolves. One wolf is evil — he is fear, anger, rage, envy, sorrow, regret, greed, arrogance, self-pity, guilt, resentment, inferiority, lies, false pride, competition, superiority, and ego.

The other is good — he is love, joy, greatness, peace, hope, sharing, serenity, humility, kindness, benevolence, friendship, empathy, generosity, truth, compassion and faith.

This same fight is going on inside you, and inside every other person, too."

They thought about it for a minute, and then one child asked his grandfather, "Which wolf will win, Grandfather?"

The elder simply replied, "The one you feed."

Adapted from various versions on the internet.

Ponder this:

We have two natures within us, both struggling for mastery. It is your choice as to which nature will dominate.

A Leader Always Fails Upwards!

Abraham Lincoln was born in a log cabin. The fact that he went on to become President — and to lead the United States through the most difficult period of its history — is truly remarkable. It is even more amazing when you consider what it took to be an important leader in the middle of the nineteenth century. Although we hear a lot about people like Lincoln or Andrew Jackson or Ulysses S. Grant — people who came from nothing to wield great power — these were most definitely the exceptions that disproved the rule. Moreover, the rule was, most successful people started out with all the advantages. Financially, it was much harder to get rich a hundred and fifty years ago than it is today — and if you failed, it was much harder to get back on your feet. There was no safety net from the government or from anywhere else to make sure that you did not go hungry. In those days, it was every man for himself.

With that in mind, let's look for a minute at some of the things that Lincoln faced and overcame. You have probably seen lists similar to this, describing Lincoln's failures, but I'd like to go through it again in order to make some important points, which we will take up immediately after the list. As you are reading this list, I'd like you also to think of setbacks you have faced in your own life, and how you responded to them.

In 1832, Lincoln was working in a general store in Illinois when he decided to run for the state legislature. However, the election was some months away, and before it took place, the general store went bankrupt and Lincoln was out of a job. So, he joined the army and served three months. When he got out, it was time for the election — which he lost.

Then, with a partner, Lincoln opened a new general store. His partner embezzled from the business, and the store went broke. In addition, shortly thereafter, the partner died, leaving Lincoln with debts that took several years to pay off.

In 1834, Lincoln ran again for the state legislature, and this time he won. He was even elected to three more terms of two years each. During this period, however, Lincoln also suffered some severe emotional problems. Today he would have been categorized as clinically depressed.

By 1836, Lincoln had become a licensed attorney. At that time, a law degree was not required to pass the bar exam, and Lincoln had been studying on his own for years. He later became a circuit-riding lawyer, traveling from county to county in Illinois to plead cases in different jurisdictions. He was one of the most diligent of all the lawyers doing this kind of work, and between 1849 and 1860 he missed only two court sessions on the circuit.

In 1838, he was defeated in an attempt to become Speaker of the Illinois legislature, and in 1843, he was defeated in an attempt to win nomination for Congress. In 1846, he was elected to Congress, but in 1848, he had to leave because his party had a policy of limiting terms. In 1854, he was defeated in a run for the U.S. Senate. In 1856, he lost the nomination for Vice President, and in 1858, he was again defeated in a race for the Senate. Yet in spite of all these setbacks, in 1860 he was elected President of the United States.

Every time Lincoln failed at something, he was soon trying for something even bigger. After he lost his seat in the state legislature, he ran for the national congress. After he lost a bid for the Senate, he tried to become vice president – and after he lost the Senate race again, he ended up President of the whole country.

Lincoln saw himself as a leader long before anyone else did – and this is the first key to his leadership genius. He may have failed many times, but somehow he always failed upward. He was propelled by a sense of mission, and he was willing and able to do whatever it took to get that great mission accomplished.

~ Dr. Tony Alessandra

Ponder this:

The road to success is strewn with many casualties who simply did not have the tenacity to persist in the face of failure… after failure. Lincoln had the hide of a champion.

The Elephant Who Lost an Eye

An elephant came to the edge of a stream of clear rushing water. Being thirsty, the elephant leaned over, dropped its trunk into the cool water and... plunk!

"What? What happened?" the elephant cried. "I can't see! My eye... it fell in the water! Oh nooooooh," the elephant wailed in a panic, "I lost my eye!"

And, in fact, the elephant's right eye had popped out of its socket and fallen into the stream. The elephant searched frantically for the eye, groping with its trunk along the bottom of the stream. The more he groped, the cloudier the water became. That made him panic even more, and he started churning up great piles of sand, until he couldn't see anything.

Then the elephant heard the sound of laughing. Furious, he looked around to see who it was, and saw a little green frog sitting on a log, laughing and laughing.

"You think this is funny?" the elephant shouted. "I lose an eye and that makes you laugh?"

"What's funny is to see how upset you are. Calm down and everything will be fine," the frog replied.

The elephant felt a little ashamed and took the frog's advice. He stopped moving his trunk around, and soon the water became clearer as the sand sank to the bottom. And there in the stream lay his eye. He reached for it with his trunk and popped it back into its socket. And then he thanked the frog.

(M Vishal, 2014)

Ponder this:

This simple parable contains great wisdom. There's nothing funny about losing an eye... the sudden panic, thrashing around in murky water, desperation... that's exactly what happens to us when we lose control and panic. Our haste makes us blind.

We become temporarily incapable of seeing the world around us objectively and rationally. But there is an antidote to panic: wait. Wait until the situation becomes clear and the black clouds disperse.

Basketball Experiment

Visualization plays a key role in the successes of many great athletes. Physiologist Edmund Jacobson found that when he had subjects visualize certain athletic activities, amazingly it affected and sharpened their muscles. He discovered subtle but very real movements in the muscles that corresponded to the movement the muscles would make if they were really performing the imagined activity.

Further research revealed that a person who consistently visualizes a certain physical skill develops "muscle memory" which helps him when he physically engages in the activity. A related study by Australian psychologist Alan Richardson confirmed the reality of the phenomenon.

Richardson chose three groups of students at random. None had ever practised visualization. The first group practised free throws every day for twenty days. The second made free throws on the first day and the twentieth day, as did the third group. But members of the third group spent 20 minutes every day visualizing free throws. If they "missed," they "practised" getting the next shot right.

On the twentieth day Richardson measured the percentage of improvement in each group. The group that practised daily improved 24 percent. The second group, unsurprisingly, improved not at all. The third group, which had physically practised no more than the second, did twenty-three percent better—almost as well as the first group!

In his paper on the experiment, published in Research Quarterly, Richardson wrote that the most effective visualization occurs when the visualizer feels and sees what he is doing. In other words, the visualizers in the basketball experiment "felt" the ball in their hands and "heard" it bounce, in addition to "seeing" it go through the hoop.

(Randolph, 2002)

Ponder this:

Scientists conducting serious objective research have discovered that the human nervous system does not distinguish between actual actions and imaginary actions. In other words, your brain has the same perception of events whether you toss the ball into the basket or just imagine in detail that you do.

So, to make visualization work, it is not enough to just "see" what was happening; it is necessary to feel the experience and to imagine every tiny detail. This way you can fool your brain into believing that the imaginary event really occurred.

Bruce Lee - Wisdom of Yoda

A master martial artist asked Bruce to teach him everything Bruce knew about martial arts. Bruce held up two cups, both filled with liquid.

"The first cup," said Bruce, "represents all of your knowledge about martial arts. The second cup represents all of my knowledge about martial arts. If you want to fill your cup with my knowledge, you must first empty your cup of your knowledge.

(Lee, 2007)

Ponder this:

According to Yoda (Star Wars), to advance in life, "you must unlearn what you have learned". Oftentimes, to learn something new, it is necessary to first abandon old ways of doing things.

The Ben Hogan Comeback

There is a story about the legendary professional golfer Ben Hogan that exemplifies the way all champions think, regardless of their profession. In 1954, Hogan was playing in a tournament during the early part of the season somewhere in Texas. The weather conditions were absolutely horrible. It was cold, pouring rain and windy. Under today's rules the tournament wouldn't even have been played, but back in the 1950's things were different. Despite the frigid conditions, Hogan played one of the best rounds of his life, a full five shots lower than the rest of the field. After handing in his score card and drying his clubs, he promptly started right back towards the practice ground. A young reporter, eager to get an angle on the mythical man, hurried out after him. He caught him just as Hogan was getting set to hit his first shot on the range and Hogan give him a steely glare as he asked, "Mr. Hogan you have just played a spectacular round in appalling conditions. Why then have you come back out in the rain after you had such an excellent game?"

Without looking up, Hogan began to hit shots towards his damp and distant caddie, he then growled his reply, "I practise because I hope to play just as well again tomorrow as I did today."

Hogan's story is particularly interesting.

In 1949 he was involved in a catastrophic automobile accident. However, before the actual collision, Hogan saved his wife, Valerie from serious injury by throwing himself over her at the last second, but his own legs were crushed.

Blood clots rising from his injured legs toward his lungs and brain threatened his life.

When they got him to the hospital, the doctors told his wife, "Mrs Hogan, your husband will not survive the night." His wife quietly said, "You obviously don't know my husband."

He underwent a risky operation and the next morning he proved the experts wrong and was able to continue with his life. However, for an extended period in hospital, Hogan barely clung to life and at times the Chief Surgeon, Alton Oschner felt he was losing the battle against a series of menacing and life threatening blood clots that had reached Hogan's lungs. Importantly, he pulled through, but they told his wife, "Mrs Hogan, Ben is never going to walk again", and she said, "You obviously don't know my husband."

As the months went by, Ben began to get his spirit back again. Although he realized that he was in a hospital bed with his body badly damaged, he decided that he was going to play golf again. The doctors were astounded when they learnt of his intent and they said to his wife, "Mrs Hogan, Ben now wants his golf clubs strung up on the ceiling where he can see them all day long, but he is never going to play golf again" and Mrs Hogan said, "You obviously don't know my husband."

With much difficulty and incredibly painful physical therapy, he was back on the course within 10 months. His damaged legs had to be swathed in elastic to keep the swelling down, and he limped as he walked, but, incredibly, he was soon winning major tournaments again. During the period of 1950-1953, Hogan scaled the golfing heights even more successfully than before the accident and won the bulk of his nine major titles. In 1953, he won three of the four majors — the U.S. and British Opens and the Masters. And he remained the dominant player in the game until the dawn of the '60s.

Adapted from various versions on the internet.

Ponder this:

The argument of 'greatest ever' will never be settled, but Ben Hogan remains the most ruthlessly accurate 'shotmaker' the golfing world has ever known.

Building a Beautiful Heart

One day a young man, a stranger, who shone with the vigour of youth, came to the town square, gathered all the people around and proclaimed, "Listen folks! Look at my heart! Isn't it is the most beautiful heart in this whole valley!"

The large crowd, who was attracted by his charisma and bold words, could not but admire his heart — for it was indeed perfect. There was not a mark or a flaw in it. They just nodded their heads in complete agreement; it truly was the most beautiful heart they had ever seen.

The young man was now swimming in pride; he was over the top with excitement as everyone was praising his personality, and especially his heart. Now he raised his voice even more and asserted, "Dear folks! You are looking at the most beautiful of this entire region!" And the audience vociferously cheered him, except one old man.

This senior gentleman, slightly bent in the back, but whose face radiated serenity, approached this young man and said, "Why, your heart is not nearly as beautiful as mine."

At this point, many in the crowd actually started laughing, because the old man's heart indeed looked very odd. It was beating strongly, no doubt, but was full of scars; it had places where pieces had been removed and other pieces put in here and there, which didn't fit quite right and there were too many jagged edges around the outside of the heart. In fact, in some places there were deep gouges where whole pieces were missing. It was really a pathetic sight to behold, completely contrary to the beautiful heart of the young man.

Several in the crowd thought the old man was probably out of his mind, because there was no way one could compare his heart with that of the young man. And now the young man himself laughed sarcastically and said, "Grandpa! I know you are kidding! Just look at my heart, how perfect it is!"

The old man then gently replied, "Yes, my dear young man, yours is a gorgeous one, however I would never trade mine with yours." Everyone around now became inquisitive; the noise level reduced considerably. When there was a semblance of silence, the old man continued in a soft and tempered tone, "You see, every scar in my heart represents a person to whom I have given my love — I tear out a piece of my heart and give it to them, and often they give me a piece of their heart too which fits into the empty place in my heart. But because the pieces aren't exact, I have some rough edges. But I love them and in fact cherish them, because they remind me of the love we shared."

The old man was now quiet for a while, and then smiled and continued, "You know, there have been times when I have given pieces of my heart away, and the other person hasn't returned anything back to me. These are the empty gouges — giving love is taking a chance. Although these deep holes are painful, they stay open, reminding me always of the love I have for these people, and I hope someday they may return and fill the space I have waiting."

He then fixed his gaze upon the young man and remarked gravely, "So now do you see what true beauty and love is, dear young man?"

The proud youth slowly felt his pride being washed away by the tears running silently down his cheeks. He felt humbled by the simple wisdom that the old teacher had bestowed on him. He walked up to the old man, and stood in front of him. He then reached into his perfect, young and beautiful heart, and with a loud cry he ripped out a piece of his precious heart. With trembling hands and teary eyes, he presented it to the old man.

The wise old man accepted his offering, placed it in his heart and then lovingly took a piece from his old and scarred heart and placed it in the newly created wound in the young man's heart. It did fit the place, but not perfectly, as there were some misshapen edges.

After this instant, the young man looked at his heart; it was not perfect anymore, but he was not sad. For, though not of the perfect shape as before, his heart was now more beautiful and more fulfilling than ever since love from the old man's heart now flowed into his. He felt more whole as new life coursed through his soul.

The next moment, the two men embraced and started to walk quietly side by side. The crowd too was speechless; they just silently made way for the two. It was too profound and powerful a lesson to sink in easily; everyone who was a witness to this could not but start reflecting about the status of their own hearts…and how they could at least from that moment onwards try to make it more beautiful in a true way.

(Baba, 2009)

Ponder this:

For a heart to be called a heart it must be filled with compassion. If we say we have a heart, let it show in small or big but genuine acts of kindness. For, when we do this, whether we are of any substantial help to the other person or not, we would surely have benefited ourselves as we will begin to experience a joy that is absolutely incomparable to anything else in this world.

God Answers A Call For Help

A man was caught in the raging waters of a flood. He was a god-faring man. He believed and trusted in God. God had answered his prayers and come to his aid many times in his life. There was no doubt in his mind that God will always be there for him.

Now he was in trouble … again. Again, his faith was strong. He prayed to God. He said, "God, save me. Please save me." He prayed hard. It seemed that God acknowledged his prayers because as he was bobbing up and down in the water, a big log drifted slowly alongside him. He could easily have grabbed hold of it, but he didn't. Convinced that God would have a better plan for him, he simply let it pass. He continued to pray hard again. And, yet again God answered. This time a man in a rubber dinghy called to him: "Hop aboard and I'll take you to safety." Having a phobia for small boats, the drowning man said, "No, you carry on. I'll get motion sickness." Too risky to hang around in the raging waters, the man in the dinghy shook his head and left.

Knowing that God had never let him down before, the drowning man looked up at the sky and prayed in earnest. He said, "God, I can't keep afloat much longer, Where are you?" Amazingly, as he looked up and prayed, a "black dot" appeared in the sky. The dot got bigger as it got closer to him. He recognised it. It was a helicopter. Within seconds it was directly above him. The pilot lowered a ladder and shouted, "Grab hold of the ladder and we'll pull you up".

Gasping for breath, the drowning man shouted back, "No, you go on. I'll be OK. God will save me." Bewildered, the helicopter pilot left. Sadly, the man missed his last ride to safety, and drowned.

When he entered the Pearly Gates, he met God. He looked at God in disbelief and said, "God, where were you? Why didn't you save me?"

God, perplexed, replied, "I tried. I sent you the log, but you ignored it, so I sent you the rubber dinghy. You were still not satisfied, so I sent you a helicopter. You rejected even that. What more did you want?"

Adapted from various versions on the internet.

Ponder this:

In life, there are enough times when we are disappointed, depressed or annoyed and we blame God for our unfavourable circumstances. This can be read as "GOD IS NO WHERE" or as "GOD IS NOW HERE". God appears invisible, but comes to us plainly in the things of this world. Everything depends on how you see it.

The Emperor and the Seed

An emperor in the Far East was growing old and knew it was time to choose his successor. Instead of choosing one of his assistants or his children, he decided something different. He called young people in the kingdom together one day. He said, "It is time for me to step down and choose the next emperor. I have decided to choose one of you."

The kids were shocked! But the emperor continued. "I am going to give each one of you a seed today. One very special seed. I want you to plant the seed, water it and come back here one year from today with what you have grown from this one seed. I will then judge the plants that you bring, and the one I choose will be the next emperor!"

One boy named Ling was there that day and he, like the others, received a seed. He went home and excitedly told his mother the story. She helped him get a pot and planting soil, and he planted the seed and watered it carefully. Every day he would water it and watch to see if it had grown. After about three weeks, some of the other youths began to talk about their seeds and the plants that were beginning to grow.

Ling kept checking his seed, but nothing ever grew. Three weeks, 4 weeks, 5 weeks went by. Still nothing. By now, others were talking about their plants but Ling didn't have a plant, and he felt like a failure. Six months went by-still nothing in Ling's pot. He just knew he had killed his seed.

Everyone else had trees and tall plants, but he had nothing. Ling didn't say anything to his friends, however. He just kept waiting for his seed to grow.

A year finally went by and all the youths of the kingdom brought their plants to the emperor for inspection. Ling told his mother that he wasn't going to take an empty pot, but his mother insisted that he be honest about what had happened. Ling felt sick to his stomach, but he knew his mother was right. He took his empty pot to the palace. When Ling arrived, he was amazed at the variety of plants grown by the other youths. They were beautiful-in all shapes and sizes. Ling put his empty pot on the floor and many of the other kinds laughed at him. A few felt sorry for him and just said, "Hey nice try."

When the emperor arrived, he surveyed the room and greeted the young people. Ling just tried to hide in the back. "My, what great plants, trees and flowers you have grown," said the emperor. "Today, one of you will be appointed the next emperor!" All of a sudden, the emperor spotted Ling at the back of the room with his empty pot. He ordered his guards to bring him to the front. Ling was terrified. "The emperor knows I'm a failure! Maybe he will have me killed!"

When Ling got to the front, the Emperor asked his name. "My name is Ling," he replied. All the kids were laughing and making fun of him. The emperor asked everyone to quiet down. He looked at Ling, and then announced to the crowd, "Behold your new emperor! His name is Ling!" Ling couldn't believe it. Ling couldn't even grow his seed. How could he be the new emperor?

Then the emperor said, "One year ago today, I gave everyone here a seed. I told you to take the seed, plant it, water it, and bring it back to me today. But I gave you all boiled seeds which would not grow. All of you, except Ling, have brought me trees and plants and flowers. When you found that the seed would not grow, you substituted another seed for the one I gave you. Ling was the only one with the courage and honesty to bring me a pot with my seed in it. Therefore, he is the one who will be the new emperor!"

(The Emperor And The Seed, 2011)

Ponder this:

Ling's seed wasn't meant to grow. Instead, it was meant to reveal the true character of its owner. The seed wasn't meant to blossom—the child was meant to blossom. Ling's honesty was revealed, a trait that is essential for being a successful emperor in charge of the lives of thousands of people. By revealing Ling's character, the seed blossomed in unimaginable ways.

Build Bridges, Not Fences

Once upon a time two brothers who lived on adjoining farms fell into conflict.

It was the first serious rift in 40 years of farming side by side, sharing machinery, and trading labor and goods as needed without a hitch. Then the long collaboration fell apart. It began with a small misunderstanding and it grew into a major difference, and finally it exploded into an exchange of bitter words followed by weeks of silence.

One morning there was a knock on John's door. He opened it to find a man with a carpenter's toolbox. "I'm looking for a few days of work" he said. "Perhaps you would have a few small jobs here and there I could help with? Could I help you?

"Yes," said the older brother. "I do have a job for you. Look across the creek at that farm. That's my neighbor, in fact, it's my younger brother. Last week there was a meadow between us and he took his bulldozer to the river levee and now there is a creek between us.

Well, he may have done this to spite me, but I'll go him one better. See that pile of lumber by the barn? I want you to build me a fence, an 8-foot fence, so I won't need to see his place or his face anymore."

The carpenter said, "I think I understand the situation. Show me the nails and the post-hole digger and I'll be able to do a job that pleases you."

The older brother had to go to town, so he helped the carpenter get the materials ready and then he was off for the day. The carpenter worked hard all that day measuring, sawing, nailing and hammering.

About sunset when the farmer returned, the carpenter had just finished his job. The farmer's eyes opened wide, his jaw dropped. There was no fence there at all. It was a bridge, a bridge stretching from one side of the creek to the other! A fine piece of work handrails and all, and the neighbor, his younger brother, was coming across, his hand outstretched. "You are quite a fellow to build this bridge after all I've said and done."

The two brothers stood at each end of the bridge, and then they met in the middle, taking each other's hand. They turned to see the carpenter hoist his toolbox on his shoulder.

"No, wait! Stay a few days. I've a lot of other projects for you," said the older brother.

"I'd love to stay on," the carpenter said, "but, I have many more bridges to build."

Adapted from various versions on the internet.

Ponder this:

Nurture your relationships with others. Build "bridges", not fences — one leads to openness, the other to isolation.

Whining Dog

A young lady walking down the street happened to notice an old man sitting on his porch with his dog whining incessantly. Finding it somewhat strange, she stopped and asked the old man why his dog was whining.

"Because he is sitting on a nail" replied the man.

"Then why doesn't he get up", asked the young lady.

"Because it doesn't hurt enough" said the owner.

Adapted from various versions on the internet.

Ponder this:

If you have time to whine about something that's bothering you, then you have the time to do something about it.

Perspective: It's Funny How Things Change

Dr Norman Vincent Peale, an Ohio-born preacher and author of the mega-bestseller, *The Power of Positive Thinking,* tells a story of a man who phoned him one day, deeply depressed and looking for help. Peale invited the man to his office for a chat, during which the man told him he had nothing to live for anymore.

"Everything is gone, hopeless," the man told him. "I'm living in deepest darkness. In fact, I've lost heart for living altogether."

Peale smiled sympathetically at the distraught man sitting before him. "Let's take a look at your situation," he said, taking out a sheet of paper and drawing a line down the middle of the paper. He told the man on the left side they would list the things he'd lost in his life, and on the right, the things he had remaining.

"You won't need that column on the right side," said the man sadly. "I have nothing left, period."

Peale asked, "When did your wife leave you?"

"What do you mean? She hasn't left me. My wife loves me!"

"That's great!" said Peale enthusiastically. "Then that will be number one in the right-hand column—Wife hasn't left. Now, when were your children jailed?"

"What?" the man asked, surprised. "My children aren't in jail!"

"Good! That's number two in the right-hand column—Children not in jail," said Peale, jotting it down.

After a few more questions in the same vein, the man finally got the point and smiled in spite of himself. "Funny, how things change when you think of them that way," he said.

Adapted from various versions on the internet.

Ponder this:

Don't get frustrated with your problems. Learn to re-frame how you look at various situations and you'll be amazed to see how your perspective can change.

The Obstacle in Our Path

In ancient times, a king had a boulder placed on a roadway. Then he hid himself and watched to see if anyone would remove the huge rock. Some of the king's wealthiest merchants and courtiers came by and simply walked around it. Many loudly blamed the king for not keeping the roads clear, but none did anything about getting the big stone out of the way.

Then a peasant came along carrying a load of vegetables. On approaching the boulder the peasant laid down his burden and tried to move the stone to the side of the road. After much pushing and straining, he finally succeeded.

As the peasant picked up his load of vegetables, he noticed a purse lying in the road where the boulder had been. The purse contained many gold coins and a note from the king indicating that the gold was for the person who removed the boulder from the roadway.

The peasant learned what many others never understood. Every obstacle presents an opportunity to improve one's condition.

Adapted from various versions on the internet.

Ponder this:

In life, we are presented with an "obstacle" or two from time to time. We can blame others and complain about it or, like the farmer, we can take responsibility for it is a matter of choice. If we are wise and choose to take up responsibility for the obstacle presented to us, we are sure to find "gold" in dealing with the obstacle!

Every obstacle presents an opportunity to improve our condition.

Don't Waste Your Life

In 1977, a 63-year-old grandmother named Laura Schultz heard screaming from the driveway. Her grandson had been playing with the car and accidentally released the emergency brake. The car rolled onto his arm. She was a petite woman and said she had never lifted a thing over 50 pounds in her life. Yet she lifted the 2,000 pound car off to release her grandson's arm.

After the incident, she was reluctant to speak about it with anyone. After reading her story in the National Enquirer, Dr Charles Garfield, author of Peak Performance managed to obtain an interview with her.

Laura said she didn't like talking about the event because it challenged her beliefs about what she could and could not do. She said, "If I was able to do this when I didn't think I could, what does that say about the rest of my life? Have I wasted it?"

The story has a happy ending. Garfield convinced her that her life wasn't over yet and that she could do whatever she wanted to do. He asked her what her passion was. She said that she had always loved rocks. She wanted to study geology, but her parents could not afford to send both her and her brother to college, so her brother was given preference over her. At 63, with a little coaxing from Charles Garfield, she decided to go back to school to study geology. She eventually got her degree and went to teach at a local community college.

Adapted from various versions on the internet.

Ponder this:

Don't wait until 63 to decide that you can do anything you want. Don't waste your life. Know that you are capable of much more.

The Parable of Brother Leo

A legend tells of a French monastery known throughout Europe for the extraordinary leadership of a man known only as Brother Leo. Several monks began a pilgrimage to visit Brother Leo to learn from him. Almost immediately, they began to bicker about who should do various chores.

On the third day they met another monk going to the monastery, and he joined them. This monk never complained or shirked a duty, and whenever the others would fight over a chore, he would gracefully volunteer and do it himself. By the last day, the others were following his example, and from then on they worked together harmoniously.

When they reached the monastery and asked to see Brother Leo, the man who greeted them laughed.

'But our brother is among you!' And he pointed to the fellow who had joined them late in the trip.

(Michael, 2012)

Ponder this:

The parable about Brother Leo teaches another model of leadership, where leaders are preoccupied with serving rather than being followed, with giving rather than getting, and doing rather than demanding. It's a form of leadership based on example, not command. It's called 'servant-leadership'.

The Strange Glowing Force

Two boys, in their early teens were hiking through a wooded area on the way back to their small village when they discovered a cave that a hermit made home. They had travelled very far and still had a long way to go before they returned home. They were hungry and tired and looking for a place to stay for the night.

When they saw the hermit, they started to run off.

He beckoned to them to stay for a while. He didn't get many visitors and enjoyed company when the opportunity permitted. They started to make an excuse, but he persuaded them to stay. So he invited them to dinner, and asked them of their journey and of the people and things they had encountered. The two boys enjoyed talking to the old man and were glad they had stayed. The food was very good and they were warm.

After the old man cleaned up from dinner, they sat around the fire, drank tea and continued to talk. The old man then said, "I have something for you boys," and went off into the cave. He came back out with a very old wooden box. He sat down between the boys on the ground crossing his legs in front of him. He placed the box in his lap and then looked first at the boy on his right, then turned to look at the boy on his left.

They both smiled, as he looked at them, and wondered what could be in the box.

He lifted the latch and slowly opened the box. To the amazement of both boys, they saw a strange glowing force. It was vaguely ball shaped, yet had no apparent substance. However, the old man lifted it out of the box and held it in his hand.

"Here" he said, "I want both of you to have some of this" and he broke two large pieces off, leaving a very small piece, which he put back into the box. He then gave each piece of the strange mysterious object to the boys.

One of the boys said, "You have given us so much that you have little left."

The man replied, "It will grow back." He then added, "This is a very magical and powerful thing that I give to you. For if you break off a piece and give it to everyone you meet it will grow. If you do not give it away it will shrink and eventually fade away to nothing."

The boys looked at each other with an expression of doubt and skepticism in their faces. But they were appreciative and thanked the man. It had already been arranged that they would spend the night and boys went off to bed.

The next morning, the smell of breakfast woke the two boys. Knowing they had to leave, the Hermit prepared a simple meal that would hold them until they could return home later in the afternoon. He let them refill their water and gave them some jerky in case the breakfast wasn't enough. They thanked him again and went on their way.

Once the boys got home, they told their families of the man and the strange gift they had each been given. Both boys made boxes for their gift. The first boy did as the stranger suggested and gave a piece of his to each of this family. The other boy did not. He kept it to himself and refused to give any of it away, even when asked for some.

As the years went by, each boy would show this gift to everyone they would meet. All who saw it marveled at it. The first boy continued to give part of his away and over the years it had grown and grown. Several times, he had made larger and larger boxes to keep it in. He gave it to everyone he met, including business associates, strangers and even the woman who became his wife. Each time, he told the story of the hermit and the cave and passed along the instructions to share this fascinating gift. Eventually, his had grown so much that he could not contain it. It consumed his home, his neighborhood and the entire countryside. In fact, he couldn't travel away from it. It seemed to always be around him.

The other did not. He kept his all to himself. He would show it to strangers and when they asked about it or tried to touch it, he would slam the lid shut on the box and return it to its shelf. He did not realize that each time he held it back without giving a piece of it away, it would get smaller.

Eventually, he went to the box and opened it, to find that his gift had disappeared. One day he happened to meet the other who was with him the day they received the gift. He was somewhat resentful when they met. The man who had always given his away, stood tall and had the look of a successful business man, while he looked old and tired. Still, the successful man asked him how he had been all these years and was genuinely interested in hearing his stories.

But the second man bitterly stated, "I regret the day that old fool gave us that horrible thing. It's done nothing but wreck my life. After all these years, someone broke into my room and stole it, but I'm glad to be rid it of it. It's caused me nothing but misery."

"I don't understand." said the first man. "Did you not give it away as the hermit suggested?"

"I did not for if I had done that, I wouldn't have any left for myself."

"But now it's gone anyway, isn't it?" said the first man. "Here I will give you a piece of mine and you can have another start. You see, this gift we were given such a long time ago was not mysterious at all. What it is, is FRIENDSHIP and you have to give it away to get some back in return."

~ Christian Godefroy

Ponder this:

Life is abundant. Have an abundance mindset and you will be blessed accordingly.

A Lesson in Goal Achievement

In 1950, Japan, war-torn and with no natural resources of its own, set a goal to become the number one nation in the world in the manufacture of textiles. They were committed and were willing to do whatever it took. At the end of that decade, they achieved their goal. They were the world's leaders in the production of textiles.

In 1960, they set another goal — to become the world's number 1 manufacturer of steel. Now, here's the "absurdity" of their goal: Japan had no iron ore of its own. You might ask, "Who in the right mind would set a goal such as this?" Well Japan did. They had to import iron ore from other countries, build steel mills, manufacture the steel, and then ship it all over the world. Yeah, crazy! Perhaps, especially when one considers the transportation costs involved. They knew this, but it did not deter them. They had a goal, and they were committed to it. At the end of that decade, they had reached their goal, and were the world's number 1 manufacturer of steel.

They then set a goal for the next decade, the 1970s. This goal was to become the world's number 1 producer of automobiles. They worked hard. Sadly, they did not make it. They missed the goal by one year, having attained it in 1980.

They set a goal for the 1980's — to be the world's number 1 nation in the producer of electronics and computers. The results speak for themselves. More than 90% of the TV sets used in America today, are made in Japan.

~ Unknown

Ponder this:

Goals, work for individuals, families, teams, organisations, and nations. The success of any organisation/nation is the collective commitment of its people.

The Pipeline Story

There was once a small mountain village where the natives were dependent upon a spring in the centre of their village. One day the spring suddenly ran dry. There was another spring and reservoir a few miles away but it was too far for the villagers to travel.

The village leaders called an emergency meeting to discuss the issue. Two villagers offered to take on the task of delivering water to the village on a daily basis. The elders awarded independent contracts to each of them. They felt that a little competition would keep prices low and ensure a backup supply of water.

The first of the two people, Ed, immediately ran out, bought two galvanized steel buckets and began running back and forth along the trail to the reservoir.

He immediately began making money as he labored morning till dusk hauling water from the reservoir with his two buckets. He would empty them into the large concrete holding tank the villagers had built.

Each morning he arose much earlier than the rest of the villagers to make sure there was enough water to meet their morning needs. It was hard work, but he was very happy to be making money and for having one of the two exclusive contracts for this business.

The second winning contractor, Bill, disappeared for a while. He was not seen for months, which made Ed very happy since he had no competition. Ed was making all the money.

Instead of buying two buckets to compete with Ed, Bill had created a plan, found four investors, and returned six months later with a construction crew. Within a year his team had built a large volume stainless steel pipeline, which connected the village holding tank to the reservoir.

At the grand opening celebration, Bill announced that his water was cleaner than Ed's water. Bill knew that there had been complaints about dirt in Ed's water.

Bill also announced that he could supply the village with water 24 hours a day, seven days a week. Ed could only deliver water on the weekdays. He did not work on weekends.

Then Bill announced that he would charge 75% less than Ed did for this higher quality and more reliable supply. The village cheered and ran immediately for the faucet at the end of Bill's pipeline.

In order to compete, Ed also lowered his rates by 75%, bought two more buckets, added covers to his buckets, and began hauling four buckets each trip. In order to improve his service, he employed his two sons to give him a hand for the night shift and on weekends.

Bill, the pipeline builder, however, began enjoying the fruits of his labor. He drastically reduced his work hours and began enjoying the income his venture generated. He found the pipeline required minimal maintenance, so he was free to spend his days fishing the mountain streams and enjoying time with his kids.

Many years later, after both men had died, the pipeline was still an integral part of village life and the pipeline builder's children continued to enjoy the benefits of their father's entrepreneurial spirit.

(Kiyosaki, 2000)

Ponder this:

Work smarter, not necessarily harder.

The Story of the Pencil

A boy was watching his grandmother write a letter. At one point, he asked, 'Are you writing a story about what we've done? Is it a story about me?'

His grandmother stopped writing her letter and said to her grandson, 'I am writing about you, actually, but more important than the words is the pencil I'm using. I hope you will be like this pencil when you grow up.'

Intrigued, the boy looked at the pencil. It didn't seem very special. 'But it's just like any other pencil I've ever seen!'

'That depends on how you look at things. It has five qualities which, if you manage to hang on to them, will make you a person who is always at peace with the world.'

'First quality, you are capable of great things, but you must never forget that there is a hand guiding your steps. We call that hand God, and He always guides us according to His will.'

'Second quality, now and then, I have to stop writing and use a sharpener. That makes the pencil suffer a little, but afterwards, he's much sharper. So you, too, must learn to bear certain pains and sorrows, because they will make you a better person.'

'Third quality, the pencil always allows us to use an eraser to rub out any mistakes. This means that correcting something we did is not necessarily a bad thing; it helps to keep us on the road to justice.'

'Fourth quality, what really matters in a pencil is not its wooden exterior, but the graphite inside. So always pay attention to what is happening inside you.'

'Finally, the pencils fifth quality, it always leaves a mark. In just the same way, you should know that everything you do in life will leave a mark, so try to be conscious of that in your every action.'

(Coelho, 2009)

Ponder this:

No matter how simple a person may appear on the outside, great abilities lie within.

The Monkey Trap

In many countries with large monkey populations, the natives have devised a very effective method of trapping monkeys. The plan is deceptively simple: the natives take a gourd (a typically large fruit with a hard skin e.g. a coconut) or some similar object and cut a hole just large enough for a monkey's hand to pass through; they add some extra weight to the gourd with sand or pebbles, then put a nut or some fruit inside and place the gourd where a monkey will find it.

Here's what happens: the monkey sticks his hand through the hole to get the food — but with the prize in its grasp, the monkey cannot get its hand back out. The hole is too small for the monkey's closed fist to pass through and the gourd is too heavy for the creature to carry. Because the monkey will not let go of its prize, it becomes trapped. The animal gives up its freedom to hold on to a small piece of food.

To escape, all the monkey needs to do is let go of the bait, but because it views the treat as its possession and is not willing to let go, the monkey remains trapped.

Clearly it's not the coconut that's the trapping the monkey. Rather the true trap is in the monkey's own mind — it's attachment to its possession and unwillingness to "Let Go."

Adapted from various versions on the internet.

Ponder this:

The monkey is acting out of instinct; it probably doesn't have the ability to recognize the danger of holding on to the bait. However, humans should be able to avoid falling into such a trap. We should be able to understand the folly of holding on to things that don't serve us well, but we often put our attachment to possessions ahead of our own well-being.

The Parable of the Twin Fetuses

Once upon a time, twin boys were conceived.

Weeks passed and the twins developed within the womb. As their awareness grew, they laughed for joy: "Isn't it great that we were conceived? Isn't it great to be alive? "

Together the twins explored their world. When they found their mother's cord that gave them life, they sang for joy! "How great our mother's love is, that she shares her own life with us!"

As weeks stretched into months, the twins noticed how much each was changing.

"What does it mean?" one asked.

"It means our stay in this world is drawing to an end." said the other.

"But I don't want to leave this world," said one. "I want to stay here always."

"We have no choice," said the other. "But maybe there is life after birth."

"But how can there be?" responded one. "We will shed our life cord and how can life be possible without it? Besides, we have seen evidence that others were here before us, and none of them has returned to tell us there is life after birth. No, this is the end. Maybe there is no mother after all."

"But there has to be," protested the other. "How else did we get here? How do we remain alive?"

"Have you ever seen our mother?" said one.

"Maybe she only lives in our minds. Maybe we made her up because the idea made us feel good."

So the last days in the womb were filled with deep questioning and fear.

Finally, the moment of birth arrived. When the twins had passed from their world of the womb, they opened their eyes and cried for joy — for what they saw exceeded their wildest expectations.

~ Unknown

Ponder this:

A great story symbolizing change. Change is the only constant in our lives. Embrace it and expect the best.

The Ripple Effect

The Master was walking through the fields one day when a young man, with a troubled look upon his face, approached him.

"On such a beautiful day, it must be difficult to stay so serious," the Master said.

"Is it? I hadn't noticed," the young man said, turning to look around and notice his surroundings. His eyes scanned the landscape, but nothing seemed to register; his mind elsewhere. Watching intently, the Master continued to walk.

"Join me if you like." The Master walked to the edge of a still pond, framed by sycamore trees, their leaves golden orange and about to fall.

"Please sit down," the Master invited, patting the ground next to him. Looking carefully before sitting, the young man brushed the ground to clear a space for himself.

"Now, find a small stone, please," the Master instructed.

"What?"

"A stone. Please find a small stone and throw it in the pond."

Searching around him, the young man grabbed a pebble and threw it as far as he could.

"Tell me what you see," the Master instructed.

Straining his eyes to not miss a single detail, the man looked at the water's surface. "I see ripples."

"Where did the ripples come from?"

"From the pebble I threw in the pond, Master."

"Please reach your hand into the water and stop the ripples," the Master asked.

Not understanding, the young man stuck his hand in the water as a ripple neared, only to cause more ripples. The young man was now completely baffled. Where was this going? Had he made a mistake in seeking out the Master? After all he was not a student, perhaps he could not be helped? Puzzled, the young man waited.

"Were you able to stop the ripples with your hands?" the Master asked.

"No, of course not."

"Could you have stopped the ripples, then?"

"No, Master. I told you I only caused more ripples."

"What if you had stopped the pebble from entering the water to begin with?" The Master smiled such a beautiful smile; the young man could not be upset.

"Next time you are unhappy with your life, catch the stone before it hits the water. Do not spend time trying to undo what you have done. Rather, change what you are going to do before you do it." The Master looked kindly upon the young man.

"But Master, how will I know what I am going to do before I do it?"

"Take the responsibility for living your own life. If you're working with a doctor to treat an illness, then ask the doctor to help you understand what caused the illness. Do not just treat the ripples. Keep asking questions."

The young man stopped, his mind reeling. "But I came to you to ask you for answers. Are you saying that I know the answers?"

"You may not know the answers right now, but if you ask the right questions, then you shall discover the answers."

"But what are the right questions, Master?"

"There are no wrong questions, only unasked ones. We must ask, for without asking, we cannot receive answers. But it is your responsibility to ask. No one else can do that for you."

(Fares, 2011)

Ponder this:

Life is all about the choices we make. Choices have consequences – good or bad. To mitigate unfavourable consequences, ask questions. Questions are the answers. Importantly, if you ask better questions, you'll get better answers!

The Praying Hands

Back in the fifteenth century, in a tiny village near Nuremberg, lived a family with eighteen children. Eighteen! In order merely to keep food on the table for this big family, the father and head of the household, a goldsmith by profession, worked almost eighteen hours a day at his trade and any other paying chore he could find in the neighbourhood.

Despite their seemingly hopeless condition, two of Albrecht Durer's children had a dream. They both wanted to pursue their talent for art, but they knew full well that their father could never afford to send either of them to Nuremberg to study at the Academy.

After many long discussions at night in their crowded bed, the two boys finally worked out a pact. They would toss a coin. The loser would go down into the nearby mines and, with his earnings, support his brother while he attended the academy. Then, when that brother who won the toss completed his studies, in four years, he would support the other brother at the academy, either with sales of his artwork or, if necessary, also by labouring in the mines.

They tossed a coin on a Sunday morning after church. Albrecht Durer won the toss and went off to Nuremberg.

Albert went down into the dangerous mines and, for the next four years, financed his brother, whose work at the academy was almost an immediate sensation. Albrecht's etchings, his woodcuts, and his oils were far better than those of most of his professors, and by the time he graduated, he was beginning to earn considerable fees for his commissioned works.

When the young artist returned to his village, the Durer family held a festive dinner on their lawn to celebrate Albrecht's triumphant homecoming. After a long and memorable meal, punctuated with music and laughter, Albrecht rose from his honoured position at the head of the table to drink a toast to his beloved brother for the years of sacrifice that had enabled Albrecht to fulfil his ambition. His closing words were, "And now, Albert, blessed brother of mine, now it is your turn. Now you can go to Nuremberg to pursue your dream, and I will take care of you."

All heads turned in eager expectation to the far end of the table where Albert sat, tears streaming down his pale face, shaking his lowered head from side to side while he sobbed and repeated, over and over, "No ...no ...no ...no."

Finally, Albert rose and wiped the tears from his cheeks. He glanced down the long table at the faces he loved, and then, holding his hands close to his right cheek, he said softly, "No, brother. I cannot go to Nuremberg. It is too late for me. Look ... look what four years in the mines have done to my hands! The bones in every finger have been smashed at least once, and lately I have been suffering from arthritis so badly in my right hand that I cannot even hold a glass to return your toast, much less make delicate lines on parchment or canvas with a pen or a brush. No, brother ... for me it is too late."

More than 450 years have passed. By now, Albrecht Durer's hundreds of masterful portraits, pen and silver point sketches, watercolours, charcoals, woodcuts, and copper engravings hang in every great museum in the world, but the odds are great that you, like most people, are familiar with only one of Albrecht Durer's works. More than merely being familiar with it, you very well may have a reproduction hanging in your home or office.

One day, to pay homage to Albert for all that he had sacrificed, Albrecht Durer painstakingly drew his brother's abused hands with palms together and thin fingers stretched skyward. He called his powerful drawing simply "Hands," but the entire world almost immediately opened their hearts to his great masterpiece and renamed his tribute of love "The Praying Hands."

(Mandino, 1990)

Ponder this:

No one is completely independent. No one makes it alone. We all need help. Express gratitude for the help you have received for your achievements in life.

The Best Religion

A brief dialogue between Brazillian theologist Leonardo Boff and the Dalai Lama.

Here is what Boff, one of the renovators of the Theology of Freedom, recounts of this remarkable encounter:

In a round table discussion about religion and freedom in which the Dalai Lama and myself were participating at recess, I maliciously, and also with interest, asked him,

"Your holiness, what is the best religion?"

Boff anticipated that the Dalai Lama's response would be Tibetan Buddhism or one of the other Eastern religions that are far older than Christianity.

The Dalai Lama paused, smiled and looked me in the eyes … which surprised me because I knew of the malice contained in my question. He answered,

"The best religion is the one that gets you closest to God. It is the one that makes you a better person."

To get out of my embarrassment with such a wise answer, I asked,

"What is it that makes me better?"

Dalai Lama's response was even more enlightening:

"Whatever makes you more compassionate, more sensible, more detached, more loving, more humanitarian, more responsible, more ethical. The religion that will do that for you is the best religion."

I was silent for a moment, marveling and even today, thinking of his wise and irrefutable response.

"I am not interested, my friend, about your religion or if you are religious or not. What really is important to me is your behavior in front of your peers, family, work, community, and in front of the world. Remember, the universe is the echo of our actions and our thoughts."

"The law of action and reaction is not exclusively for physics. It is also of human relations. If I act with goodness, I will receive goodness. If I act with evil, I will get evil. You will always have what you desire for others. Being happy is not a matter of destiny. It is a matter of options."

Finally he said,

"Take care of your thoughts because they become words; words because they become actions; actions because they become habits. Habits will form your character; character will form your destiny; and your destiny will be your life. *There is no religion higher than the truth.*"

(Sykes, 2010)

Ponder this:

It is how we act, whether we are persons of integrity and authenticity, how we think about others and ourselves, that is more important than our religion and religious beliefs. To the extent it assists us successfully in leading a good life, we can say our religion is "the best."

The Value of Time

Imagine there is a bank that credits your account each morning with $86,400.
It carries over no balance from day to day.
Every evening the bank deletes whatever part of the balance you failed to use during the day. What would you do?

Draw out every cent, of course!

Each of us has such a bank. Its name is TIME.
Every morning, it credits you with 86,400 seconds.
Every night it writes off, as lost, whatever of this you have failed to invest to good purpose.
It carries over no balance.
It allows no overdraft.
Each day it opens a new account for you.
Each night it burns the remains of the day.
If you fail to use the day's deposits, the loss is yours.
There is no going back.
There is no drawing against the "tomorrow."
You must live in the present on today's deposits.
Invest it so as to get from it the utmost in health, happiness, and success!
The clock is running.

To realize the value of **one year**, ask a student who failed a grade.
To realize the value of **one month**, ask a mother who gave birth to a premature baby.
To realize the value of **one week**, ask the editor of a weekly newspaper.

To realize the value of **one hour**, ask the lovers who are waiting to meet.
To realize the value of **one minute**, ask a person who missed the train.
To realize the value of **one second**, ask a person who just avoided an accident.

Keep in mind that time waits for no one.
Yesterday is history.
Tomorrow is a mystery.
Today is a gift.
Make the most of today.

Adapted from various versions on the internet.

Ponder this:

No one is so powerful that they can stop the march of time. Each new day is a privilege to us so we can start afresh. Take the advantage of a new day and make the best of it.

SAT Score

This is a true story about a young man from a small town who graduated from high school with straight A's. He then applied to the state university for admission. As part of the admissions procedure, he had to take the Scholastic Aptitude Test, like all the applicants to the universities nationwide. A few weeks later, he received a letter from the admissions department informing him that he scored in the 99th percentile on the test and he was accepted for the fall semester.

He was happy to be accepted but there was one problem. He didn't know about percentiles and he concluded mistakenly that the 99th percentile was his IQ score. He knew that the average IQ is 100 and he felt he could never do university-level work with his 'limited' intelligence.

For the entire fall semester he failed or nearly failed every course. Finally, his counselor called him in and asked him why he was doing so poorly.

"Well", he said, "You can't blame me. I've only got a 99 IQ."

The counselor had the student's file in front of him. "Why do you say that?" he asked.

"That's what is said in my letter of admission to the university," he replied.

When the counselor realized what had happened he explained the difference between IQ and a percentile. "A

99th percentile means that you scored equal to or higher than 99 percent of all the students in America who wrote this test. You're one of the brightest kids on the campus."

When the young man realized his error and changed his belief about his intelligence, he became a different person. He went back into his classes and went to work with a new sense of competence and confidence. By the end of the semester he was on the honor roll and he eventually graduated on the top 10 of his class.

(Tracy, 1993)

Ponder this:

Most of us act in a way that is congruent with our innermost beliefs – good or bad. Rid yourself of limiting beliefs and you'll realize your true potential.

Wright Brothers

On December 17, 1903, two brothers from Dayton, Ohio, with no formal engineering training, defied gravity in their curious flying machine over the dunes of North Carolina's remote Outer Banks. By making what many consider the first powered, sustained and controlled manned airplane flights, Orville and Wilbur Wright ushered in the era of flight and soared into history.

Wilbur and Orville were the sons of Milton and Susan Wright and members of a warm, loving family that encouraged learning and doing.

Their dream started with an idea that was planted in their minds by a toy given to them by their father. In the words of the boys, "Late in the autumn of 1878, our father came into the house one evening with some object partly concealed in his hands, and before we could see what it was, he tossed it into the air. Instead of falling to the floor, as we expected, it flew across the room till it struck the ceiling, where it fluttered awhile, and finally sank to the floor." This simple toy made of cork, bamboo and paper and powered by a rubber band mesmerized the boys and sparked their passion for aviation.

The Wright brothers were great thinkers. They enjoyed learning new things. Initially, they recycled broken parts, built a printing press and opened their own printing office. In 1894, Wilbur and Orville were caught up in the bicycling craze that swept the nation. To augment the income from their printing trade, they began repairing and selling bicycles. This soon grew into a full-time business, and in 1896 they began to manufacture their own bikes. The Wright Cycle Company returned a handsome profit, but the brothers cared little about the money. They were already thinking about trading their wheels for wings.

The tight-knit brothers, born four years apart, were wedded to their work; Wilbur told reporters that he didn't have time for both a wife and an airplane.

The brothers spent many hours researching, testing their machines and making improvements after unsuccessful attempts at human flight. What started out as a hobby soon became a passion. With determination and patience they realized their dream in 1903 when they made the first sustained, controlled flights in a powered aircraft which they named the Wright Flyer.

While the 1903 Wright Flyer did indeed fly, it was underpowered and difficult to control. For two years they made flight after flight, fine tuning the controls, engine, propellers, and configuration of their airplane. At first, they could only fly in a straight line for less than a minute. But by the end of 1905, they were flying figure-eight's over Huffman Prairie, staying aloft for over half an hour, or until their fuel ran out. The 1905 Wright Flyer was the world's first practical airplane.

The next time you hear or see an airplane or travel on one, remember where it all started. A simple idea conceived in the minds of two young men who did not finish high school. Believe it or not, they did not have a University degree in Aeronautical Engineering, Mathematics, Physics or any other subject. They were not scientists in the true sense of the word. In fact, many of their peers who did not witness their accomplishment, had trouble believing that two bicycle mechanics from Dayton, Ohio did what they claimed.

The Wright Brothers' had a cause and they would not give up; they never let failure or a setback discourage them. When knocked down, they made no excuses; they got back up on their feet and kept going. They epitomized the Samurai saying "Fall seven times and stand up eight". The Wright brothers were models of integrity. Let's learn from them.

Adapted from various versions on the internet.

Ponder this:

To achieve noteworthy success in life, find something you are passionate about and dedicate your life to it just as the Wright Brothers did.

Steve Jobs - Stay Hungry, Stay Foolish

I am honored to be with you today at your commencement from one of the finest universities in the world. I never graduated from college. Truth be told, this is the closest I've ever gotten to a college graduation. Today I want to tell you three stories from my life. That's it. No big deal. Just three stories.

The first story is about connecting the dots.

I dropped out of Reed College after the first 6 months, but then stayed around as a drop-in for another 18 months or so before I really quit. So why did I drop out?

It started before I was born. My biological mother was a young, unwed college graduate student, and she decided to put me up for adoption. She felt very strongly that I should be adopted by college graduates, so everything was all set for me to be adopted at birth by a lawyer and his wife. Except that when I popped out they decided at the last minute that they really wanted a girl. So my parents, who were on a waiting list, got a call in the middle of the night asking: "We have an unexpected baby boy; do you want him?" They said: "Of course." My biological mother later found out that my mother had never graduated from college and that my father had never graduated from high school. She refused to sign the final adoption papers. She only relented a few months later when my parents promised that I would someday go to college.

And 17 years later I did go to college. But I naively chose a college that was almost as expensive as Stanford, and all of my working-class parents' savings were being spent on my college tuition. After six months, I couldn't see the value in it. I had no idea what I wanted to do with my life and no idea how college was going to help me figure it out. And here I was spending all of the money my parents had saved their entire life. So I decided to drop out and trust that it would all work out OK. It was pretty scary at the time, but looking back it was one of the best decisions I ever made. The minute I dropped out I could stop taking the required classes that didn't interest me, and begin dropping in on the ones that looked interesting.

It wasn't all romantic. I didn't have a dorm room, so I slept on the floor in friends' rooms, I returned coke bottles for the 5¢ deposits to buy food with, and I would walk the 7 miles across town every Sunday night to get one good meal a week at the Hare Krishna temple. I loved it. And much of what I stumbled into by following my curiosity and intuition turned out to be priceless later on. Let me give you one example:

Reed College at that time offered perhaps the best calligraphy instruction in the country. Throughout the campus every poster, every label on every drawer, was beautifully hand calligraphed. Because I had dropped out and didn't have to take the normal classes, I decided to take a calligraphy class to learn how to do this. I learned about serif and san serif typefaces, about varying the amount of space between different letter combinations, about what makes great typography great. It was beautiful, historical, artistically subtle in a way that science can't capture, and I found it fascinating.

None of this had even a hope of any practical application in my life. But ten years later, when we were designing the first Macintosh computer, it all came back to me. And we designed it all into the Mac. It was the first computer with beautiful typography. If I had never dropped in on that single course in college, the Mac would have never had multiple typefaces or proportionally spaced fonts. And since Windows just copied the Mac, it's likely that no personal computer would have them. If I had never dropped out, I would have never dropped in on this calligraphy class, and personal computers might not have the wonderful typography that they do. Of course it was impossible to connect the dots looking forward when I was in college. But it was very, very clear looking backwards ten years later.

Again, you can't connect the dots looking forward; you can only connect them looking backwards. So you have to trust that the dots will somehow connect in your future. You have to trust in something — your gut, destiny, life, karma, whatever. This approach has never let me down, and it has made all the difference in my life.

My second story is about love and loss.

I was lucky — I found what I loved to do early in life. Woz and I started Apple in my parent's garage when I was 20. We worked hard, and in 10 years Apple had grown from just the two of us in a garage into a $2 billion company with over 4000 employees. We had just released our finest creation — the Macintosh — a year earlier, and I had just turned 30.

And then I got fired. How can you get fired from a company you started? Well, as Apple grew we hired someone who I thought was very talented to run the company with me, and for the first year or so things went well. But then our visions of the future began to diverge and eventually we had a falling out. When we did, our Board of Directors sided with him. So at 30 I was out. And very publicly out. What had been the focus of my entire adult life was gone, and it was devastating.

I really didn't know what to do for a few months. I felt that I had let the previous generation of entrepreneurs down – that I had dropped the baton as it was being passed to me. I met with David Packard and Bob Noyce and tried to apologize for screwing up so badly. I was a very public failure, and I even thought about running away from the valley. But something slowly began to dawn on me – I still loved what I did. The turn of events at Apple had not changed that one bit. I had been rejected, but I was still in love. And so I decided to start over.

I didn't see it then, but it turned out that getting fired from Apple was the best thing that could have ever happened to me. The heaviness of being successful was replaced by the lightness of being a beginner again, less sure about everything. It freed me to enter one of the most creative periods of my life.

During the next five years, I started a company named NeXT, another company named Pixar, and fell in love with an amazing woman who would become my wife. Pixar went on to create the world's first computer animated feature film, Toy Story, and is now the most successful animation studio in the world. In a remarkable turn of events, Apple bought NeXT, I returned to Apple, and the technology we developed at NeXT is at the heart of Apple's current renaissance. And Laurene and I have a wonderful family together.

I'm pretty sure none of this would have happened if I hadn't been fired from Apple. It was awful tasting medicine, but I guess the patient needed it. Sometimes life hits you in the head with a brick. Don't lose faith. I'm convinced that the only thing that kept me going was that I loved what I did. You've got to find what you love. And that is as true for your work as it is for your lovers. Your work is going to fill a large part of your life, and the only way to be truly satisfied is to do what you believe is great work. And the only way to do great work is to love what you do. If you haven't found it yet, keep looking. Don't settle. As with all matters of the heart, you'll know when you find it. And, like any great relationship, it just gets better and better as the years roll on. So keep looking until you find it. Don't settle.

My third story is about death.

When I was 17, I read a quote that went something like: "If you live each day as if it was your last, someday you'll most certainly be right." It made an impression on me, and since then, for the past 33 years, I have looked in the mirror every morning and asked myself: "If today were the last day of my life, would I want to do what I am about to do today?" And whenever the answer has been "No" for too many days in a row, I know I need to change something.

Remembering that I'll be dead soon is the most important tool I've ever encountered to help me make the big choices in life. Because almost everything — all external expectations, all pride, all fear of embarrassment or failure — these things just fall away in the face of death, leaving only what is truly important. Remembering that you are going to die is the best way I know to avoid the trap of thinking you have something to lose. You are already naked. There is no reason not to follow your heart.

About a year ago I was diagnosed with cancer. I had a scan at 7:30 in the morning, and it clearly showed a tumor on my pancreas. I didn't even know what a pancreas was. The doctors told me this was almost certainly a type of cancer that is incurable, and that I should expect to live no longer than three to six months. My doctor advised me to go home and get my affairs in order, which is doctor's code for prepare to die. It means to try to tell your kids everything you thought you'd have the next 10 years to tell them in just a few months. It means to make sure everything is buttoned up so that it will be as easy as possible for your family. It means to say your goodbyes.

I lived with that diagnosis all day. Later that evening I had a biopsy, where they stuck an endoscope down my throat, through my stomach and into my intestines, put a needle into my pancreas and got a few cells from the tumor. I was sedated, but my wife, who was there, told me that when they viewed the cells under a microscope the doctors started crying because it turned out to be a very rare form of pancreatic cancer that is curable with surgery. I had the surgery and I'm fine now.

This was the closest I've been to facing death, and I hope it's the closest I get for a few more decades. Having lived through it, I can now say this to you with a bit more certainty than when death was a useful but purely intellectual concept:

No one wants to die. Even people who want to go to heaven don't want to die to get there. And yet death is the destination we all share. No one has ever escaped it. And that is as it should be, because Death is very likely the single best invention of Life. It is Life's change agent. It clears out the old to make way for the new. Right now the new is you, but someday not too long from now, you will gradually become the old and be cleared away. Sorry to be so dramatic, but it is quite true.

Your time is limited, so don't waste it living someone else's life. Don't be trapped by dogma – which is living with the results of other people's thinking. Don't let the noise of others' opinions drown out your own inner voice. And most important, have the courage to follow your heart and intuition. They somehow already know what you truly want to become. Everything else is secondary.

When I was young, there was an amazing publication called The Whole Earth Catalog, which was one of the bibles of my generation. It was created by a fellow named Stewart Brand not far from here in Menlo Park, and he brought it to life with his poetic touch. This was in the late 1960's, before personal computers and desktop publishing, so it was all made with typewriters, scissors, and Polaroid cameras. It was sort of like Google in paperback form, 35 years before Google came along: it was idealistic, and overflowing with neat tools and great notions.

Stewart and his team put out several issues of The Whole Earth Catalog, and then when it had run its course, they put out a final issue. It was the mid-1970s, and I was your age. On the back cover of their final issue was a photograph of an early morning country road, the kind you might find yourself hitchhiking on if you were so adventurous. Beneath it were the words: "Stay Hungry. Stay Foolish." It was their farewell message as they signed off. Stay Hungry. Stay Foolish. And I have always wished that for myself. And now, as you graduate to begin anew, I wish that for you.

Stay Hungry. Stay Foolish.

(Yarow, 2011)

Ponder this:

This is the text of the Commencement address by Steve Jobs, CEO of Apple Computer and of Pixar Animation Studios, delivered on June 12, 2005.

A Blessing in Disguise

In the northern frontier of ancient China, there lived a man who was particularly skilled in raising horses. People knew of him and called him Sai Ong – literally "Old Frontiersman."

One day, for some unknown reason, his horse got loose and ran off into the Hu territory beyond the Great Wall. The Hu tribes were hostile toward the Chinese, so everyone assumed the horse was as good as lost.

Horses were very valuable to the people living at the frontier, so they regarded this loss as a great financial setback. They visited Sai Ong to express their sympathies, but Sai Ong's elderly father surprised them by remaining calm and unaffected. Much to their puzzlement, the old man asked: "Who says this cannot be some sort of blessing?"

Months later, the horse returned to the stable with a companion – a fine steed of the Hu breed. It was as if Sai Ong's wealth suddenly doubled. Everyone came by to marvel at the new horse and to congratulate him, but again his elderly father showed no great emotions. He said: "Who says this cannot be some sort of misfortune?"

Sai Ong's son enjoyed riding and took the new horse out for a ride. An accident occurred, causing him to fall badly and break a leg. Again sympathetic people came to console the family, and again they saw that the grandfather remained as calm as ever. Just like before, he told them: "Who says this cannot be some sort of blessing?"

One year later, the Hu people amassed and crossed the border into China. All the able-bodied young men were summoned into the army to take up arms in defense. Fierce battles ensued, resulting in heavy casualties. Among the inhabitants of the northern frontier, nine out of ten men died.

Sai Ong's son did not go into battle due to his broken leg. Because of this, he was spared that terrible fate, and his family survived the war intact.

Thus, blessings may turn out to be misfortunes, and misfortunes blessings. They change from one to the other endlessly; the workings of destiny has a truly fathomless depth.

(Major, Queen, Meyer, & Roth, 2010)

Ponder this:

Every dark cloud has a silver lining or, as chapter 58 of Tao Te Ching expresses it:

Misfortune is what fortune depends upon
Fortune is where misfortune hides beneath

True Friends

Out along a country lane is a field with two horses in it. From a distance, each looks like every other horse. But if one is walking by, one will notice something quite amazing.

Looking into the eyes of one horse will disclose that he is blind. His owner has chosen not to have him put down, but has made a good home for him. This alone is amazing, but close observation will reveal something even more amazing.

Listening closely, one will hear the sound of a bell. Looking around for the source of the sound, one will see that it comes from the smaller horse in the field. Attached to her bridle is a small bell. It lets her blind friend know where she is, so he can follow her.

As one stands and watches these two friends, one sees how she is always checking on him and that he will listen for her bell and then slowly walk to where she is, trusting that she will not lead him astray.

Like the owners of these two horses, God does not throw us away just because we are not perfect or because we have problems or challenges. He watches over us and even brings others into our lives to help us when we are in need.

Sometimes we are the blind horse being guided by the little ringing bell of those who God places in our lives.

Other times we are the guide horse, helping others see. True friends are like this; you don't always see them, but you know they are always there.

Adapted from various versions on the internet.

Ponder this:

A true friend is one who supports and stands by you in times of need; who makes your problem his/her problem, just so you don't have to deal with it on your own.

True Love – Past, Present and Future

It was about 8:30 am on a busy morning when an elderly gentleman in his 80's arrived to have the stitches removed from his thumb. He stated that he was in a hurry as he had an appointment at 9:00am.

I took his vital signs and had him take a seat, knowing it would be over an hour before someone would be able to attend to him. I saw him looking at his watch and decided, since I was not occupied with another patient, I would take a look at his wound.

On examination, it was well healed, so I talked to one of the doctors and got the necessary materials to remove his sutures and redress his wound.

While taking care of his wound, we engaged in conversation. I enquired if his next appointment was medically related as he was anxious to be on time. He said 'no'; he needed to go to the nursing home to eat breakfast with his wife.

I then inquired about her health. He told me that she had been there for a while and that she had Alzheimer's disease. As I finished dressing his wound, I asked if she would be worried if he was a bit late. He replied that she no longer knew who he was; that she had not recognized him for the past five years.

I was surprised, and asked, "And you still go every morning, even though she doesn't know who you are?"

He smiled as he patted my hand and said, "She doesn't know me, but I still know who she is."

I had to hold back my tears as he left. I had goose bumps on my arm, and thought "That is the kind of love I want in my life."

Adapted from various versions on the internet.

Ponder this:

True love transcends the physical. True love is an acceptance of all that is, has been, will be, and will not be.

Bad Temper

There was a little boy with a bad temper. His father gave him a bag of nails and told him that every time he lost his temper, to hammer a nail in the back fence. The first day the boy had driven 37 nails into the fence. Then it gradually dwindled down. He discovered it was easier to hold his temper than to drive those nails into the fence. Finally the day came when the boy didn't lose his temper at all. He told his father about it and the father suggested that the boy now pull out one nail for each day that he was able to hold his temper. The days passed and the young boy was finally able to tell his father that all the nails were gone. The father took his son by the hand and led him to the fence. You have done well, my son, but look at the holes in the fence. The fence will never be the same.

When you say things in anger, they leave a scar just like this one. A verbal wound is as bad as a physical one.

Adapted from various versions on the internet.

Ponder this:

Be careful what you say in anger. Words, once spoken, cannot be taken back. Many a spirit has been broken and many a relationship has been destroyed by harmful words that penetrate the human soul. Hearts when broken through words carelessly spoken are the hardest things to repair!

The Fisherman

A boat docked in a tiny Mexican village.

An American tourist complimented the Mexican fisherman on the quality of his fish and asked how long it took him to catch them.

"Not very long," answered the Mexican.

"But then, why didn't you stay out longer and catch more?" asked the American.

The fisherman smiled again and said, "This is plenty here for my family right now. Some of the fish we can eat, and the others we can sell or trade for the other things we need."

"But it's not even lunchtime. What do you do with the rest of your time?"

"In the morning," the fisherman explained, "I like to sleep late. When I wake I fish a little, mostly just for the pleasure of fishing. In the afternoon I play with my children and take siesta with my wife. In the evenings I have dinner with my family. And then, when my children are sleeping, I stroll into the village, where I sip wine and play guitar with my friends."

The American scoffed and said, "I'm a Harvard MBA and I can help you."

The fisherman was a little skeptical, but nonetheless he obliged and asked, "How?"

"You should fish longer every day," the American counseled, "late into the afternoon. This way you will catch more fish and make more money, and you can buy a bigger boat. With the bigger boat you will catch even more fish, make even more money, and then you can buy another boat and hire another man to work the second boat."

"But what then?" the fisherman inquired.

"Oh, we are just getting started! With two boats you'll catch even more fish and make even more money, and before you know it, you'll have a whole fleet of boats and every man in the village looking for work will come to you."

"But what then?" the fisherman asked.

"Before too long, you can cut out the middleman, sell your fish direct to the cannery, and make more money. As your fleet of boats continues to expand, you can build your own cannery. And before you know it, you'll be able to leave this small coastal village, move to Mexico City, and manage your expanding enterprise."

"But what then?" the fisherman asked.

"Before too long, you can cut out the middleman, sell your fish direct to the cannery, and make more money. As your fleet of boats continues to expand, you can build your own cannery. And before you know it, you'll be able to leave this small coastal village, move to Mexico City, and manage your expanding enterprise."

"But what then?" the fisherman persisted.

"Well then, you can begin to ship your fish to different parts of the world. Down into Asia and Australia and up into North America. And as demand grows for your fish, you can leave Mexico City, move to Los Angeles, open a distribution plant there, and begin to ship your fish to Europe and every corner of the globe."

"But what then?" the fisherman asked again.

The American continued, "By then your business will be one of the great ventures of the industry. You can move to New York City and manage your empire from the epicenter of the business world."

"How long will all this take?" the fisherman asked.

"Twenty-five, maybe thirty years," the banker explained.

"But what will I do then?" the fisherman asked.

The American's eyes lit up like a Christmas tree. "That's the best part," he said. "When the time is just right, you can go down to Wall Street, list your business as a public company, offer an IPO, and make millions and millions of dollars."

"Millions?" the fisherman asked.

"More money than you ever dreamed you could earn in ten lifetimes," the American explained.

"But what then?" the fisherman asked.

The American did not know what to say. He had reached his climax. He was stumped. But then a thought crossed his mind and triggered an idea, and he turned once more to the fisherman and spoke.

"Well then, you could move to a small coastal village. . . . You could sleep late. . . . You could fish just for the pleasure of fishing. . . . In the afternoons, you could take siesta with your wife. . . . In the evenings, you could have dinner with your family . . . and then you could stroll into the village and sip wine and play guitar and sing songs with your friends. . . ."

Adapted from various versions on the internet.

Ponder this:

While success has its rewards, sometimes we need to put our work into perspective and see the bigger picture.

The Triple-Filter Test

In ancient Greece, Socrates was reputed to hold knowledge in high esteem. One day an acquaintance met the great philosopher and said, "Do you know what I just heard about your friend?"

"Hold on a minute," Socrates replied. "Before you talk to me about my friend, I'd like you to pass a little test. It's called the Triple Filter Test. The first filter is Truth. Have you made absolutely sure that what you are about to tell me is true?"

"Well, no," the man said, "actually I just heard about it and…"

"All right," said Socrates. "So you don't really know if it's true or not. Now, let's try the second filter, the filter of Goodness. Is what you are about to tell me about my friend something good?"

"No, on the contrary…"

"So," Socrates continued, "you want to tell me something bad about him, but you're not certain it's true. You may still pass the test though, because there's one filter left – the filter of Usefulness. Is what you want to tell me about my friend going to be useful to me?"

"No, not really."

"Well," concluded Socrates, "if what you want to tell me is neither true, nor good, nor even useful, why tell it to me at all?"

Adapted from various versions on the internet.

Ponder this:

Remember that saying, "If you don't have something nice to say about someone, then don't say it".

You Are a Masterpiece

A crow lived in the forest and was absolutely satisfied in life.
Then, one day he saw a swan.
"The swan is so elegant and I am so plain...
"The swan must be the happiest bird in the world" he thought.

He expressed his thoughts to the swan.
"Actually," the swan replied,
"I was feeling that I was the happiest bird around until I saw a parrot, which has two colours.
"I now think the parrot is the happiest bird in creation."

The crow then approached the parrot.
The parrot explained,
"I lived a very happy life – until I saw a peacock.
"I have only two colours, but the peacock has multiple colours."

The crow then visited a peacock in the zoo and saw that hundreds of people had gathered to see him.

After the people had left, the crow approached the Peacock.

He said, "Dear Peacock,
"You are so beautiful.
"Every day thousands of people come to see you.
"When people see me, they immediately shoo me away.
"I think you must be the happiest bird on the planet."

The peacock replied,
"I always thought that I was the most beautiful and happy bird on the planet.
"But because of my beauty,
"I am entrapped in this zoo."

The peacock continued,
"I have examined the zoo very carefully,
"And I have realized that the crow is the only bird not kept in a cage.
"So for past few days I have been thinking that if I were a crow,
"I could happily roam everywhere."

Adapted from various versions on the internet.

Ponder this:

God made each of us unique masterpieces with significance and a specific purpose. Don't compare yourself with others and wish you were like them. Count your blessings and be your best self.

Thinking "Out of the Box"

A long time ago in a small Italian town, a merchant had the misfortune of owing a large sum of money to the moneylender. The moneylender, who was old and ugly, fancied the merchant's beautiful daughter so he proposed a solution. He said he would forgo the merchant's debt if he could marry the daughter. Both the merchant and his daughter were horrified by the proposal.

The moneylender told them that he would put a black pebble and a white pebble into an empty bag. The girl would then have to pick one pebble from the bag. If she picked the black pebble, she would become the moneylender's wife and her father's debt would be forgiven. If she picked the white pebble she need not marry him and her father's debt would still be forgiven. But if she refused to pick a pebble, her father would be thrown into jail.

They were standing on a pebble strewn path in the merchant's garden. As they talked, the moneylender bent over to pick up two pebbles. As he picked them up, the sharp-eyed girl noticed that he had picked up two black pebbles and put them into the bag. He then asked the girl to pick her pebble from the bag.

What would you have done if you were the girl?

Basically, she had three options:

Refuse to take a pebble.

Show that there were two black pebbles in the bag and expose the moneylender as a cheat, but the debt would remain.

Pick a black pebble and sacrifice herself in order to save her father from his debt and imprisonment.

The quick-witted girl considered her options and came up with a brilliant idea. She put her hand into the moneybag and drew out a pebble. Without looking at it, she fumbled and let it fall onto the pebble-strewn path where it immediately became lost among all the other pebbles.

"Oh, how clumsy of me," she said. "But never mind, if you look into the bag for the one that is left, you will be able to tell which pebble I picked." Since the remaining pebble is black, it must be assumed that she had picked the white one. And since the moneylender dared not admit his dishonesty, the girl changed what seemed an impossible situation into an advantageous one.

Adapted from various versions on the internet.

Ponder this:

Most complex problems do have a solution, sometimes we have to think about them in a different way.

Delay Judgement

A lovely little girl was holding two apples with both hands.

Her mum came in and softly asked her little daughter with a smile: "My sweetie, could you give your mum one of your apples?"

The girl looked up at her mum for a few seconds, then she suddenly took a quick bite on one apple, and then another quick bite on the other.

The mum felt the smile on her face freeze. She tried hard not to reveal her disappointment.

Then the little girl handed one of her bitten apples to her mum and said: "Mummy, here you are. This is the sweeter one."

Adapted from various versions on the internet.

Ponder this:

No matter who you are, how experienced you are, and how knowledgeable you think you are, always delay judgement. Give others the privilege to explain themselves. What you see may not be the reality. Never conclude for others.

A Pound Of Butter

There was a farmer who sold a pound of butter to the baker. One day the baker decided to weigh the butter to see if he was getting a pound and he found that he was not. This angered him and he took the farmer to court. The judge asked the farmer if he was using any measure. The farmer replied, "Your Honour, I am primitive. I don't have a proper measure, but I do have a scale." The judge asked, "Then how do you weigh the butter?" The farmer replied "Your Honour, long before the baker started buying butter from me, I have been buying a pound loaf of bread from him. Every day when the baker brings the bread, I put it on the scale and give him the same weight in butter. If anyone is to be blamed, it is the baker."

Adapted from various versions on the internet.

Ponder this:

We get back in life what we give to others. Whenever you take an action, ask yourself this question: Am I giving fair value for the wages or money I hope to make? Honesty and dishonesty become a habit. Some people practise dishonesty and can lie with a straight face. Others lie so much that they don't care what the truth is anymore. But, they are only deceiving themselves.

Learning from Failure

A young reporter was commissioned to interview an old and very successful entrepreneur.

"Sir," he asked politely, "what has been the secret of your success?"

The older man leaned back on his leather swivel chair, behind his shining mahogany desk, and replied, "Two words, son, two words: right decisions."

The reporter wrote it down. Then he asked another question. "And how do you learn to make right decisions, sir?"

The successful business man leaned back further and replied, "One word, son, one word: experience."

The reporter wrote this down, too, and then asked, "Well, sir, how do you acquire experience?"

The older man leaned forward over his desk and whispered conspiratorially, "Two words, son, two words: wrong decisions!"

Adapted from various versions on the internet

Ponder this:

The only real failure is failing to learn from one's mistakes.

School Yard Fight

This is a true story of an incident in my life as a young boy. At the time I didn't know I was using visualisation to manifest a particular outcome, but this story will give you an understanding of the immense power of visualization combined with emotion.

I think I was in the seventh grade at that time, so I would have been around 11 or 12 years old. In grammar school, like most other schools, we had a bully. His name was Denis Shots.

I'll never forget Denis for as long as I live because, even though we were in the same grade, I couldn't help but think that he was much older than I was. He was huge and probably the only kid in grammar school that already had hair on his chest, and to top it off, he was going a little bald.

Denis was mean and his demeanour showed it. He enjoyed intimidating other kids. Therefore, it's not surprising that I avoided him as much as possible. Besides, I don't have a big stature and I was just a little guy at grammar school.

One day it rained heavily so we remained in the classroom to have lunch. When the teacher left the classroom, Denis decided to make mischief. For some reason, he picked on me. He walked across the room to my desk, pushed me aside, grabbed the brown paper bag that contained my lunch and took it over to the window. Back in those days the schools had old-fashioned crank style windows with big hooks. Denis placed my lunch on the hook and cranked up the window.

Annoyed, I walked over to him. I had a choice. I could try to physically retrieve my lunch bag from him, or I could choose to run out of the classroom and seek some help.

At that moment I realized that my mother was in the school, working in a room down the hall on a P.T.A. project. Given that I couldn't punch him in the nose and get away with it, I chose the second option. I ran down the hall straight to my mother. She's Portuguese, 100% Portuguese and full of passion. She loves her son very much and I knew she'd fight my battle for me. She didn't let me down. She just tramped right into that classroom with me holding onto her skirt. She went right up to Denis Shots and popped him in the side of the head a few times and got my brown paper bag back for me.

However, that was not the only thing I got back that day. I also got a reputation as being the biggest pansy and sissy that anyone had ever seen in that school.

So the choice I made that day – to elicit my mother's help instead of standing up for myself – had severe consequences thereafter. I lost all my friends, not that I had many to begin with. Of course, Denis Shots continued to taunt me endlessly.

As the weeks went by, I yearned for an opportunity to redeem myself. Lo and behold, the Universe responded… as it always does. It gave me an opportunity to show that I was not the pansy or sissy that I was perceived to be.

One day, during the morning break in the playground, Denis Shots came up to me and, for no reason at all, pushed me hard. I fell to the ground. As I lay on the ground, I look up at this big chap laughing at me. I realise that unless I did something about it, Denis was going to make my life miserable for the rest of my time at this school. That was unacceptable. Without hesitation, I bounced back up on my feet, got right up to him and pushed him back with all my might. He didn't budge an inch and just laughed at me. Infuriated, close-up with my finger pointed at his face, I said to him, "That's it. I've had enough of you. You and I are going to settle this thing once and for all. I'll meet you after school behind the building."

Holy cow! I couldn't believe what I just did. I challenged Denis Shots to a fight!

This was an absolute mismatch — there was no way in the world that I could beat Denis. I had all day to envision what was going to happen that afternoon. My heart sank just thinking about it, and I couldn't get it out of my mind. The pictures going through my mind were not pleasant. All I could see was pain and more pain. I couldn't concentrate on the remaining lessons for that day. I tried to figure out how I might be able to get out of this fight. Clearly, I was in a fix. I couldn't back out without making an absolute fool of myself. I knew that I had to see this through.

The word got out and started to spread rapidly among the kids. The kids were not very encouraging, to say the least. Mostly, they'd come up to me during the breaks and say, "Hey John, I hear you are taking on Denis Shots after school. Good luck. See you there." I would give them a blank look and then silently say to myself, "Yeah, thanks for reminding me."

However, amidst all my apprehension, something unusual happened – something I wasn't consciously aware of at that time. I started to create another picture… a picture of a world without Denis Shots in it.

I realised that there was no way I could physically beat him, but if I didn't deal with this situation now, it would haunt me for the rest of my life.

So I said to myself, "I've got to do whatever I need to do to put up with whatever he throws at me. The only way I can 'win' is to show him that I will not quit, no matter how bad he hurts me. I know that if I quit, he'll keep picking on me for weeks and months and years to come. So I need to show him that, come what may, I will just not quit."

I created a vision of me being beaten, falling down and taking as much punishment as Denis could just dish out. Regardless of what he did, I saw myself getting back up again and again, facing up to him with no sign of quitting. I just played that picture in my mind over and over again. I was so consumed by the impending fight that I didn't pay much attention to any of the lessons in class that day.

Come three o'clock, we all made our way out to the back of the building. There was quite a gathering. Back in those days, there were no formalities. The kids would form a circle around the fighters and the fight would begin. Denis and I squared off immediately.

I did not know it at the time, but visualization works! What happened is exactly what I envisioned. Basically, he was hitting me, and I was hitting the ground. My attempts to strike back were in vain. I couldn't even reach him – I was hitting air. However, no matter how many times he hit me,

I kept getting up and going at him with all the strength I could muster.

Now here's the interesting part: When we first started fighting, everybody was rooting for Denis. He was the perceived champion and I was the big sissy.

However, as the fight progressed, a huge shift in energy took place. The more I kept getting up onto my feet — with swollen lips, bleeding nose, bruised hands and knees, torn shirt and soiled pants — the more the kids started rooting for me. Soon enough almost all the kids were rooting for me because they recognised my courage to take on the school bully.

Interestingly, the more the kids rooted for me, the less Denis would hit me and the softer were his blows. It wasn't long before he realized that I wasn't going to give up and that he was being perceived as a villain. To end the fight he would have to render me helpless and then face the consequences thereafter. It was a no win situation for him. Common sense prevailed and he held his hands up and said, "John, I quit. I want to be your friend."

I looked at him and said to myself, "What took you so long!" He put his arm around me and that was the beginning of a great friendship. He even became my "bodyguard" throughout my days at high school.

I share this story with you to illustrate that, even at the tender age of twelve, I was able to create a vision that allowed me to push through all the "pain" needed to manifest a favourable outcome.

~ John Kalench (Best-selling author)

Ponder this:

Perhaps, a more important lesson in this story is that if you are willing to do your part (i.e. whatever it takes), the Universe will conspire to help you.

Too Much Choice

There was an experiment conducted in 1995 by Sheena Iyengar, a professor of business at Columbia University.

In a California gourmet market, Professor Iyengar and her research assistants set up a booth of samples of Wilkin & Sons jams. Every few hours, they switched from offering an assortment of 24 bottles of jam to an assortment of just six bottles of jam. On average, customers tasted two jams, regardless of the size of the assortment, and each one received a coupon good for $1 off one Wilkin & Sons jam.

Here's the interesting part. Sixty percent of customers were drawn to the large assortment, while only 40 percent stopped by the small one. But 30 percent of the people who had sampled from the small assortment decided to buy jam, while only 3 percent of those confronted with the two dozen jams purchased a jar.

Effectively, a greater number of people bought when the assortment size was 6 than when it was 24. That study "raised the hypothesis that the presence of choice might be appealing as a theory, but in reality, people might find more and more choice to actually be debilitating."

Adapted from (Tugend, 2010)

Ponder this:

Too much choice often leads to indecision.

The NASA Experiment

Back in the early days of the space program, NASA designed an experiment to determine how its astronauts would cope without gravity, particularly with being upside down in space. NASA needed to know if the environment of space would have some unexpected negative consequences that would endanger the astronauts or their mission.

NASA scientists fitted each of the astronauts with a pair of convex goggles which turned everything they saw upside down. The astronauts had to wear the goggles 24 hours a day, 7 days per week — even when they were asleep.

Although they experienced physical symptoms of anxiety and stress initially, they gradually adapted to their new "realities." On the 26th day of the experiment, something unexpected happened. One of the astronauts was able to see things right-side up again even though he continued to wear the goggles 24 hours a day.

What the scientists discovered is that, between 26-30 days of this continuous stream of new input, one by one, all the astronauts were seeing things the right side-up despite wearing the convex goggles. Basically, each of their brains had formed enough new neural connections to turn this lie into the truth. They had literally re-created their reality!

Then NASA repeated the experiment with a slight change. This time some of the astronauts took the goggles off for a short period of time partway through the experiment. When they put the goggles back on and left them on until the 30th day, their worlds were still upside down, but when they continued on, at 26-30 consecutive days wearing the goggles, the same thing happened – everything was suddenly right-side up again.

What the scientists learned from these experiments is that the brain requires approximately 30 uninterrupted days for new neural connections to form – for new habits to form.

Adapted from various versions on the internet.

Ponder this:

Armed with this knowledge, you are now in a position to create empowering new habits. You can consciously replace a habit that is not serving you with one that will.

What Do You Make?

The dinner guests were sitting around the table discussing life. One man, a CEO, decided to explain the problem with education. He argued: "What's a kid going to learn from someone who decided his best option in life was to become a teacher?"

He said to another guest: "You're a teacher, Susan. Be honest. What do you make?"

Susan, who had a reputation of honesty and frankness, replied, "You want to know what I make?"

"I make kids work harder than they ever thought they could. I can make a C+ feel like the Congressional Medal of Honor and an A- feel like a slap in the face if the student did not do his or her very best."

"You want to know what I make?"

"I make kids wonder."

"I make them question."

"I make them criticize."

"I make them apologize and mean it."

"I make them write."

"I make them read, read, read."

"I make them show all their work in math and hide it all on their final drafts in English."

"I elevate them to experience music and art and the joy in performance, so their lives are rich, full of kindness and culture, and they take pride in themselves and their accomplishments."

"I make them understand that if you have the brains, then follow your heart…and if someone ever tries to judge you by what you make, you pay them no attention."

"You want to know what I make?"

"I make a difference."

"By the way, what do you make?"

(Mali, 2011)

Ponder this:

Teaching is the profession that makes all other professions possible!

Two seeds

Two seeds lay side by side in the fertile soil.

The first seed said, "I want to grow! I want to send my roots deep into the soil beneath me, and thrust my sprouts through the earth's crust above me … I want to unfurl my tender buds like banners to announce the arrival of spring … I want to feel the warmth of the sun on my face and the blessing of the morning dew on my petals!"

And so she grew…

The second seed said, "Hmmmm. If I send my roots into the ground below, I don't know what I will encounter in the dark. If I push my way through the hard soil above me I may damage my delicate sprouts … what if I let my buds open and a snail tries to eat them? And if I were to open my blossoms, a small child may pull me from the ground. No, it is much better for me to wait until it is safe."

And so she waited…

A yard hen scratching around in the early spring ground for food found the waiting seed and promptly ate it.

(Elan, 2014)

Ponder this:

Those of us who have worthy goals and dreams will grow and prosper. Those of us who procrastinate and refuse to risk will get eaten up by life.

Go To The ROAR!

Lions love to eat gazelle meat. But it's very difficult for lions to catch gazelles because the latter run so fast. So instead of trying to catch their quarry, a group of young lions will form a line and try to herd them in a particular direction. The gazelles easily outrun the lions, heading in the opposite direction towards supposed safety.

Except they are unknowingly being steered towards a deep, grassy area where a group of older lions are hiding. The older lions are too old and tired to be part of the chase; many are missing teeth, and would never be able to catch their own meat.

But when the gazelles are driven within close range, the old lions jump up and ROAR loudly. The startled gazelles, responding immediately to a new threat of imminent death, turn and run in the opposite direction… right back into the mouths of the young lions.

Ponder this:

Running from your fears and not facing them can often lead you into real danger and worse outcomes. In day-to-day life, the lions lying in wait may not be life threatening, but they are often false fears.

Running away may mean we remain stuck and unhappy for a long time. Optionally, we can confront the fear and move on.

Warren Buffett's 25-5 Rule

Mike Flint was Buffett's personal airplane pilot for 10 years. According to Flint, he was talking about his career priorities with Buffett when his boss jokingly said "The fact that you're still working for me, tells me I'm not doing my job. You should be out going after more of your goals and dreams."

Buffett then asked Flint to list the top 25 things he wanted to do in the next few years or even during his lifetime. Buffett then asked him to review each item and circle the top five that were most important to him. Flint was hesitant because to him they were all massively important.

But Buffett insisted that he could only pick five. So Flint spent some time with his list and after some deliberation, circled five items on his list. He then asked Flint when he planned to get to work on these top 5 and what his approach would be.

Flint said: "I'm going to get to work on them right away. I'll start tomorrow. Actually, no. I'll start tonight."

"Now once the top 5 is done," Buffett asked "what about these other 20 things on your list that you didn't circle?"

Flint replied confidently, "Well the top 5 are my primary focus, but the other 20 come in a close second. So, I'll work on those intermittently as I'm getting through my top 5."

Buffett responded sternly, "No. You've got it wrong. Everything you didn't circle just became your 'Avoid-At-All-Cost-List'. No matter what, these things get no attention from you until you've fully succeeded with your top 5."

Every behavior has a cost. Even neutral behaviors aren't really neutral. They take up time, energy, and space that could be put toward better behaviors or more important tasks.

This is why Buffett's strategy is particularly brilliant. Items 6 through 25 on our lists are important to us, but when we compare them to our top 5 goals, these items are distractions. Spending time on secondary priorities is the reason we have 25 half-finished projects instead of 5 completed ones.

Eliminate ruthlessly. Force yourself to focus. The most dangerous distractions are the ones we love, but that don't love us back.

~ Adapted from an Article in the Stable Investor

Ponder this:

The more you learn about success and what it takes to get there, the more you will see a thick, consistent thread: *when we decide to aim at less, we end up achieving more.*

The Missing Contact Lens

Brenda was a young lady who went rock climbing with some friends. This was her first rock climb.

In spite of her fear, she put on the gear, took hold of the rope, and started up the face of that enormous granite cliff. About halfway to the top, she got to a ledge where she could take a breather. As she was hanging on there, the safety rope snapped against Brenda's eye and knocked out her contact lens.

"Great", she thought. "Here I am far from home, on a rock ledge, hundreds of feet from the bottom and hundreds of feet to the top of this cliff, and now my sight is blurry." She looked and looked, hoping that it had landed on the ledge, but it just wasn't there. She was distressed and began to experience some panic, so she began praying. She prayed for calm, and asked the Lord to help her find her contact lens.

Eventually when she got to the top, a friend examined her eye and her clothing for the lens, but it was not to be found. Although she was calm now that she was at the top, she was despondent because she could not clearly see across the range of mountains. She thought of the bible verse "The eyes of the Lord run to and fro throughout the whole earth."

She thought, "Lord, You can see all these mountains. You know every stone and leaf, and You know exactly where my contact lens is. Please help me."

Later, when they had hiked down the trail to the bottom of the cliff they met another party of climbers just starting up the face of the cliff. One of them shouted out, "Hey, you guys! Anybody lose a contact lens?"

Well, that would be startling enough, but you know why the climber saw it? An ant was moving slowly across a twig on the face of the rock, carrying it!

The story doesn't end there. Brenda's father is a cartoonist. When she told him the incredible story of the ant, the prayer, and the contact lens, he drew a cartoon of an ant lugging that contact lens with the caption, "Lord, I don't know why You want me to carry this thing. I can't eat it, and it's awfully heavy. But if this is what You want me to do, I'll carry it for You."

Perhaps it would do all of us some good to say, "God, I don't know why You want me to carry this load. I can see no good in it and it's awfully heavy. But, if You want me to carry it, I will."

Adapted from various versions on the internet.

Ponder this:

When you have an intense yearning, the Universe responds in remarkable ways.

The Most Popular vs the Right Decision

A group of children were playing near two railway tracks, one still in use while the other not. Only one child played on the unused track, the rest on the operational track.

A train is approaching, and you are just beside the track interchange. You can make the train change its course to the unused track and save most of the kids. However, that would also mean the lone child playing by the unused track would be sacrificed.

Or would you rather let the train go its way?

Take a pause to think what kind of decision you could make…

Many people will choose to divert the course of the train, and sacrifice only one child. Save most of the children at the expense of only one child appears to be rational decision most people would make, morally and emotionally.

But, consider that the lone child who chose to play on the unused track had in fact made the right decision to play at a safe place. Nevertheless, he had to be sacrificed because of his ignorant friends who chose to play where the danger was.

Such kind of dilemma happens around us every day. In the office, community, in politics and especially in a democratic society; the RIGHT is often sacrificed for the interest of the majority, no matter how foolish or ignorant the majority are, and how far-sighted and knowledgeable the wise are.

Leo Velski Julian, an acclaimed critic, who told this story suggested he would not try to change the course of the train because he believed that the kids playing on the operational track were aware that the track was still in use, and that they would run away when they hear the train's sirens.

If the train was diverted, that lone child would most likely die because he never thought that a train could come over on the unused track!

Moreover, that track was not in use probably because it was not safe. If the train was diverted to such a track, we may put the lives of all passengers on board at stake! In our attempt to save few kids thinking that the train may run over them, we might end up sacrificing hundreds of people.

While we are all aware that life is full of tough decisions that need to be made, we may not realize that hasty decision may not always be the right one.

Adapted from (Jeftovic, 2013)

Ponder this:

Understand that what's right isn't always popular and what's popular isn't always right.

Gandhi's Shoes

One day, Mahatma Gandhi was running to get on a train, and as he jumped up, his shoe slipped off his foot. Though he tried to grab it, he ended up watching helplessly as it fell to the tracks. Quickly, he grabbed the other one off his foot and threw it back down the tracks towards the first rapidly disappearing shoe.

People who saw this thought perhaps Gandhi had taken leave of his senses. His response to their mystified expressions was: "At least now if a poor person finds his way across my shoe he will soon come across its mate and end up with a good pair of shoes. (Note: For most Indians back then a pair of good shoes was equivalent to a month's salary.)

~ Rav Binny Freedman

Ponder this:

If Gandhi had waited another moment, he would have lost the opportunity to turn his loss into a benefit for another. To have such an immediate reaction, a person has to reach such a level of ethical behaviour that ethics are no longer a thought out process; they become almost instinctive. Indeed it is a rare person who can develop his ethical instincts to such an extent.

One Minute Can Change a Life

He almost killed somebody, but one minute changed his life. This beautiful story comes from Sherman Rogers' old book, Foremen: Leaders Or Drivers? In his true-life story, Rogers illustrates the importance of effective relationships.

During his college years, Rogers spent a summer in an Idaho logging camp. When the superintendent had to leave for a few days, he put Rogers in charge.

"What if the men refuse to follow my orders?" Rogers asked. He thought of Tony, an immigrant worker who grumbled and growled all day, giving the other men a hard time.

"Fire them," the superintendent said. Then, as if reading Rogers' mind, he added, "I suppose you think you are going to fire Tony if you get the chance. I'd feel badly about that. I have been logging for 40 years. Tony is the most reliable worker I've ever had. I know he is a grouch and that he hates everybody and everything. But he comes in first and leaves last. There has not been an accident for eight years on the hill where he works."

Rogers took over the next day. He went to Tony and spoke to him. "Tony, do you know I'm in charge here today?" Tony grunted. "I was going to fire you the first time we tangled, but I want you to know I'm not," he told Tony, adding what the superintendent had said.

When he finished, Tony dropped the shovelful of sand he had held and tears streamed down his face. "Why he no tell me dat eight years ago?"

That day Tony worked harder than ever before – and he smiled! He later said to Rogers, "I told my wife that you first foreman in deese country who ever say, 'Good work, Tony,' and it make her feel like Christmas."

Rogers went back to school after that summer. Twelve years later he met Tony again. He was superintendent for railroad construction for one of the largest logging companies in the West. Rogers asked him how he came to California and happened to have such success.

Tony replied, "If it not be for the one minute you talk to me back in Idaho, I keel somebody someday. That one minute, changed my whole life."

Effective managers know the importance of taking a moment to point out what a worker is doing well. But what a difference a minute of affirmation can make in any relationship!

One minute. Have you got one minute to thank someone?

A minute to tell someone what you sincerely like or appreciate about him/her?

A minute to elaborate on something he did well?

One minute. It can make a difference for a lifetime.

(Sureshlasi, 2008)

Ponder this:

We should always be quick to praise excellent effort. We must not assume that people know they're appreciated and loved, but rather we are to intentionally express to them that their work is well done and we are thankful to them.

Against All Odds

In 1883, a creative engineer named John Roebling was inspired by an idea to build a spectacular bridge connecting New York with the Long Island. However bridge building experts throughout the world thought that this was an impossible feat and told Roebling to forget the idea. It just could not be done. It was not practical. It had never been done before.

Roebling could not ignore the vision he had in his mind of this bridge. He thought about it all the time and he knew deep in his heart that it could be done. He just had to share the dream with someone else. After much discussion and persuasion he managed to convince his son Washington, an up and coming engineer, that the bridge in fact could be built.

Working together for the first time, the father and son developed concepts of how it could be accomplished and how the obstacles could be overcome. With great excitement and inspiration, and the headiness of a wild challenge before them, they hired their crew and began to build their dream bridge.

The project started well, but when it was only a few months underway a tragic accident on the site took the life of John Roebling. Washington was injured and left with a certain amount of brain damage, which resulted in him not being able to walk or talk or even move.

"We told them so."
"Crazy men and their crazy dreams."
"It's foolish to chase wild visions."

Everyone had a negative comment to make and felt that the project should be scrapped since the Roeblings were the only ones who knew how the bridge could be built. In spite of his handicap Washington was never discouraged and still had a burning desire to complete the bridge and his mind was still as sharp as ever. He tried to inspire and pass on his enthusiasm to some of his friends, but they were too daunted by the task. As he lay on his bed in his hospital room, with the sunlight streaming through the windows, a gentle breeze blew the flimsy white curtains apart and he was able to see the sky and the tops of the trees outside for just a moment.

It seemed that there was a message for him not to give up. Suddenly an idea hit him. All he could do was move one finger and he decided to make the best use of it. By moving this, he slowly developed a code of communication with his wife.

He touched his wife's arm with that finger, indicating to her that he wanted her to call the engineers again. Then he used the same method of tapping her arm to tell the engineers what to do. It seemed foolish but the project was under way again.

For 13 years Washington tapped out his instructions with his finger on his wife's arm, until the bridge was finally completed. Today the spectacular Brooklyn Bridge stands in all its glory as a tribute to the triumph of one man's indomitable spirit and his determination not to be defeated by circumstances. It is also a tribute to the engineers and their team work, and to their faith in a man who was considered mad by half the world. It stands too as a tangible monument to the love and devotion of his wife who for 13 long years patiently decoded the messages of her husband and told the engineers what to do.

Perhaps this is one of the best examples of a never-say-die attitude that overcomes a terrible physical handicap and achieves an impossible goal.

Often when we face obstacles in our day-to-day life, our hurdles seem very small in comparison to what many others have to face. The Brooklyn Bridge shows us that dreams that seem impossible can be realised with determination and persistence, no matter what the odds.

(Clarita, 2011)

Ponder this:

Even the most distant dream can be realized with determination and persistence.

Expert on Religion

There is a story of a man who had done many years of scriptural study but he hadn't attained the height of spiritual progress which he was craving. He had heard that there was an enlightened master who lived on a mountain in the Himalayas. So, he travelled the great distance to find this master. When he finally reached the Guru's cave in the mountains, he was filled with excitement at being so close to attaining what he had always wanted.

When he beheld the Master, he bowed at the Master's feet and started to tell the Master everything he had studied, practiced and learned. He explained where he felt that he was stuck on his spiritual path, and all of the obstacles he faced. The Master was quiet.

When the man finished talking, the Master calmly said, "Let us have a cup of tea." "Tea?" The seeker exclaimed. "But Gurudev I have travelled weeks on foot to find you. I have spent years and years in the quest for enlightenment. I am now at your holy feet waiting for you to bestow your great wisdom upon me. I don't want tea! Just bless me with Divine Liberation."

"First we will have tea," the Master said calmly, and laid out two cups for tea. The Guru then began to pour tea, from a kettle into each cup. As he filled the seeker's cup, the man watched as the Guru poured and poured even though the tea reached to the rim of the cup. Then, still, as the cup overflowed and tea spilled onto the floor, the Guru kept pouring.

"Gurudev," the man said. "Stop. It is enough. Can you not see that the tea is now spilling out on the floor? There is no more room in the cup."

The Guru smiled and stopped pouring. "You are like this cup, my child. Just as the cup is so full that it can hold no more tea, so you are so full of your own ego, your own learning, your own stories, your own explanations, that there is no room for anything else. You cannot hold what I can teach you. Until you empty yourself of your ego, your preconceived ideas, your own book knowledge and your own explanations of how everything is, there will be no point in me teaching you at all. You cannot hold anything right now. There is no room."

(Saraswati, 2004)

Ponder this:

There are plenty of people who just read spiritual literature and assume they have come to know everything. These people have to understand that the great souls practised spiritual exercise (sadhana) for years and years before they started teaching the world. Jillellamudi Amma, a great sage of modern India, used to say ' Books never give experience, experience gives many books". Experiential knowledge always outshines bookish knowledge. Experience is ever new and book knowledge is dead and inert.

Living With Mother-in-law

A long time ago in China, a girl named Li-Li got married and went to live with her husband and mother-in-law. Within a very short period, Li-Li found that she simply couldn't get along with her mother-in-law.

Their personalities were very different, and Li-Li was angered by many of her mother-in-law's habits. In addition, she constantly criticized Li-Li.

As the weeks went by, Li-Li and her mother-in-law never stopped arguing and fighting. The situation was aggravated by the fact that, according to ancient Chinese tradition, Li-Li had to bow to her mother-in-law and obey her every wish. All the anger and unhappiness in the house caused Li-Li's poor husband great distress.

Finally, Li-Li could no longer stand her mother-in-law's bad temper and dictatorship, and she decided to do something about it.

Li-Li went to see her father's good friend, Mr. Huang, who sold various herbs and remedies.

She told him of her dilemma and asked if he would give her some poison so that she could get rid of her mother-in-law and solve the problem once and for all. Mr. Huang considered the situation carefully and finally said, "Li-Li, I will help you solve your problem, but you must listen to me and do exactly what I tell you."

Li-Li said, "Yes, Mr. Huang, I will do whatever you say."

Mr. Huang went into the back room, and returned in a few minutes with a package of herbs. He told Li-Li, "You can't use a quick-acting poison to get rid of your mother-in-law, because that would create suspicion and probably have serious consequences for her.

He said, "Therefore, I have given you a number of herbs that will slowly build up poison in her body. Every other day prepare some delicious meal and put a little of these herbs in her serving.

Also, in order to make sure that nobody suspects you when she dies you must be very careful to treat her with respect and be very friendly towards her. Don't argue with her, obey her every wish, and treat her like a queen."

Li-Li was happy with the plan. She thanked Mr. Huang and hurried home to start her plot of murdering her mother-in-law. As the months passed by, almost every other day Li-Li served the specially treated food to her mother-in-law.

She remembered what Mr. Huang had said about avoiding suspicion, so she controlled her temper, obeyed her mother-in-law, and treated her like her own mother.

After six months had passed, the atmosphere in whole household had changed. Li-Li had practiced controlling her temper to such an extent that she almost never got mad or upset.

She hadn't had an argument with her mother-in-law in six months because she now seemed much kinder and easier to get along with. By the same token, the mother-in-law's attitude toward Li-Li changed, and she began to love and treat Li-Li like her own daughter. She took every opportunity to tell friends and relatives that Li-Li was the best daughter-in-law one could ever find.

Li-Li and her mother in law were now treating each other like a real mother and daughter and Li-Li's husband was very happy to see the transformation that took place in the home.

Li-Li's relationship with her mother-in-law blossomed into one of genuine love and respect for each other. Neither would want to see the other hurt in any way. One day Li-Li abruptly stopped putting the special herbs into her mother-in-law's food, but was concerned that the damage had already been done and it would be too late to save her mother-in-law.

The next day, Li-Li rushed to see Mr. Huang and asked for his help again. She said, "Dear Mr. Huang, please help me to keep the poison from killing my mother-in-law! She's changed into such a nice woman, and I love her like my own mother. I do not want her to die because of the poison I gave her."

Mr. Huang smiled, nodded his head and said softly, "Li-Li, there's nothing to worry about. I never gave you any poison. The herbs I gave you were remedies (rich in vitamins and minerals) to improve her health. The only poison was in your mind and your attitude toward her, but that has been all washed away by the love which you gave to her."

Adapted from various versions on the internet.

Ponder this:

The practice of good deeds leads to the formation of good habits. Good habits cultivated over a long time lead to the formation of good character.

A Big Favour, please!

Dear Reader

Thank you for reading *Inspirational Short Stories About Success and Happiness*. I hope that this book has helped you in some way.

As you probably know, book lovers still look for reviews written by their peers (social proof) to help determine whether a book is worth acquiring. Unfortunately, less than 1% of consumers will review a book they have read.

To an author, reviews are GOLD! Authentic reviews tend to have a positive effect on readership. As a self-published author, I don't have the promotional muscle of a publisher behind me, so I rely on you (my readers) to help spread the word.

If you think that *Inspirational Short Stories About Success and Happiness* is worthy of your appraisal, please take a moment to write a review giving potential readers some insights into why you do (or don't) recommend the book. You will find my book listed on my author page on Amazon at http://www.amazon.com/Verusha-Singh/e/B00I4PMNSA/

Thank you so much for your support.

In gratitude,

Verusha Singh

PS. If you enjoyed the short stories in this book and would like to see how they can be used in proper context to drive home the key learning points, then I urge you to check out *The Inexplicable Laws Of Success – Discover the Hidden Truths that Separate the 'Best' from the 'Rest' (Classic Edition).*

You're Invited

If you want more of the kind of information contained in this book, join our community and receive regular doses of "The Hidden Truths", our monthly newsletter. As a reward for becoming a member you will receive a free copy of *The Ultimate Success Formula: Finally, a Formula That Reveals the Secret Behind EVERY Great Success!* as well as another surprise gift. Membership is free!

Claim your free gifts now at
www.TheInexplicableLawsOfSuccess.com/free-gifts/

Acknowledgements

We'd like to thank those who have shared with us many of the stories and anecdotes used in this book. These have been gathered over the past 20+ years from emails, newsletters, ezines, blog posts, web pages, audio clips, etc. Hence, like any book of quotations, some sources are obscure and citations are not available.

Other resources by Verusha Singh

The Inexplicable Laws Of Success – Discover the Hidden Truths that Separate the 'Best' from the 'Rest' (**Classic Edition**) available from Amazon in hardcover, softcover and e-book formats. Offering powerful insights into the reality that separate the 'Best' from the 'Rest', *The Inexplicable Laws of Success* is perhaps the first and only self-help book that provides a complete map or picture of what it takes to be truly successful in life. Using proprietary (trademarked) concepts, it explains the process of success and achievement in an unconventional yet exciting way.

PROFESSIONAL ENDORSEMENTS:

"This book gives ideas and insights into unlocking and releasing your full potential for happiness and success."

- Brian Tracy, International Best-Selling Author

The Workbook is a great self-study course to accompany the Classic Edition. It is a practical tool that guides the reader/ student through the content. The exercises are planned to help reinforce the key learning points in each chapter. For a trainer, it is a very useful reference manual and guide.

The Pocket Edition (of The Inexplicable Laws of Success) is an abridged version for readers who want the content in fewer words while retaining the essence of the original. A digital version of the Pocket Edition is not available for sale. A softcover version may be purchased from Amazon by clicking the image below.

Inspirational Words and Positive Quotes to Live By: An Insightful Collection of Motivational Quotes is packed with wisdom and

serve to remind you that life can be good, no matter what challenges you may be facing. These quotes will empower and encourage you to live your life to the fullest. They come from accomplished people, sages, philosophers and thinkers, all of whom started out as an ordinary citizens and have achieved greatness.

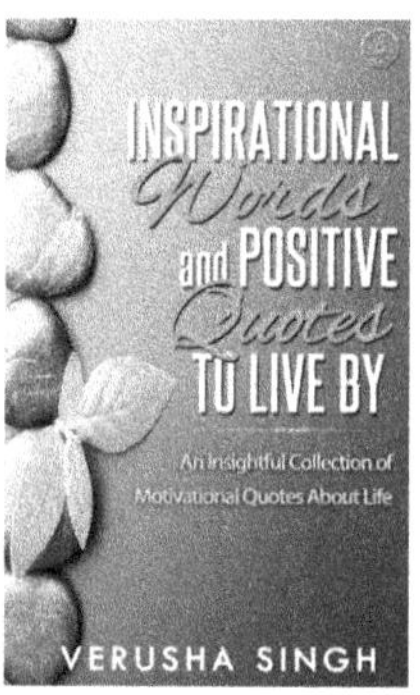

Inspirational Poems about Life and Success: Thought-provoking and Empowering Words to Uplift and Inspire You contains an impressive collection of insightful poetry that will touch your heart, give you hope and motivate you to be your best. The poems provide a powerful source of wisdom and inspiration and will make a great addition to any self-improvement or motivational book collection. It is a great resource for speakers, coaches, teachers, leaders and parents.

We all have dreams and aspirations for a better life, but for most people they remain so – just dreams and aspirations – until they die. It doesn't have to be like that. You are essentially a "goal-achieving mechanism" capable of achieving just about any outcome you set for yourself. *Accelerated Goal Achievement: An Authentic Approach to Set and Achieve Goals Faster* will help you take your dreams and turn them into concrete action plans, full of bite-sized action steps that you can confidently execute to successful completion.

About the Authors

This book is the collaborative effort of **Virend Singh**, a business professional with an MBA, and his daughter **Verusha**, a 'success writer' with a bachelor's degree in Media and Writing, and a post-graduate qualification in Editing and Publishing.

Let's Connect

- Visit www.TheInexplicableLawsOfSuccess.com
- Download free chapters of our flagship publication: The Inexplicable Laws of Success: Discover the Hidden Truths that Separate the 'Best' from the 'Rest' (Classic Edition).
- Connect with us on Facebook, Twitter, YouTube and LinkedIn via the website
- Subscribe to our newsletter – 'The Hidden Truths'
- Read our blog posts

For more resources by Verusha go to www.inkNivory.com/resources/

References

Books:

Braden, G (2006). *Secrets of the Lost Mode of Prayer: The Hidden Power of Beauty, Blessings, Wisdom, and Hurt*. San Diego: Hay House.

Chopra, D (1993). *Creating Affluence: Wealth Consciousness in the Field of All Possibilities*. New World Library Walk Your Talk With Praxis / Amber-Allen Publishing.

Halberstam, Y and Leventhal, J (1997). *Small Miracles: Extraordinary Coincidences from Everyday Life*. Adams Media Corporation. p18-19.

Hill, Napoleon (2014). *Think and Grow Rich*. CreateSpace Independent Publishing Platform. p 17

Kersey, C (1998). *Unstoppable: 45 Powerful Stories of Perseverance and Triumph from People Just Like You*. Sourcebooks, Inc.

Kiyosaki, Robert T (2000). *Rich Dad's Cashflow Quadrant: Rich Dad's Guide to Financial Freedom*. Business Plus; Later Printing edition

Major, John S, Queen, Sarah, Meyer, Andrew & Roth, D. Harold (2010). *The Huainanzi: A Guide to the Theory and Practice of Government in Early Han China (Translations from the Asian Classics)*. Columbia University Press

Mandino, Og (1990). *A Better Way to Live: Og Mandino's Own Personal Story of Success Featuring 17 Rules to Live By*. Bantam, pg 11 - 17

Murphy, J (2001). *The Power of Your Subconscious Mind*. Bantam.

Pearsall, P (1999). *The Heart's Code: Tapping the Wisdom and Power of Our Heart Energy*. Broadway Books

Vyasa, Krishna-Dwaipayana (2013). *The Complete Mahabharata (Volume 3 of 4, Books 8 to 12)*. Digireads.com

Ziglar, Zig (1975). *See You at the Top*. Pelican Books, p 199

Internet:

Alessandra, Tony Dr. *A Leader Always Fails Upwards!* Available: http://www.alessandra.com/timelytips/28.asp. Last accessed 26th August 2015.

Anonymous. *Elephant and the Blind Men*. Available: http://www.jainworld.com/literature/story25.htm. Last accessed 2nd October 2015.

Baltazar-Schwartz, Francie. *A Positive Attitude Makes Everything Different*. Available: http://www.motivateus.com/stories/attitu.htm. Last accessed 25th August 2015.

Baba, Sai. (2005). *Suitable Hiding Place*. Available: http://groups.yahoo. com/group/saibabanews/message/7356. Last accessed 3rd November 2011.

Baba, Sai. (2009). *Building a Beautiful Heart*. Available: http://media.radiosai.org/journals/Vol_08/01JAN10/09-get_inspired1.htm. Last accessed 31st August 2015.

Clarita (2011). *Inspiring Short Stories*. Available: http://www.mdjunction.com/forums/positive-thinking-discussions/general-support/2792572-inspiring-short-stories. Last accessed 12th September 2015

Coelho, Paulo. (2009). *The story of the pencil*. Available: http://paulocoelhoblog.com/2009/12/19/the-story-of-the-pencil/. Last accessed 5th September 2015.

Elan (2014). *Two Seeds (Wisdom).* Available: https://mythologystories.wordpress.com/2014/01/14/2seeds/. Last accessed 5th September 2015.

Elephant and the Blind Men. Available: http://www.jainworld.com/ literature/story25.htm. Last accessed 6th Jan 2015.

Fares, Aymen (2011*). The Ripple Effect*. Available: http://www.spiritual.com.au/2011/07/the-ripple-effect/. Last accessed 5th September 2015

Freedman, Rav Binny. *A weekly Byte ... from Isralight.* Available: http://www.isralight.org/assets/Text/RBF_kitisah06.html. Last accessed 12th September 2015

Godefroy, Christian. *The strange glowing force.* Available: http://www.hecr.tifr.res.in/~bsn/GOOD/friendship.txt, Last accessed 2nd October 2015.

Harricharan, J. *The Power of Giving*. Available: http://www.courses-free.com/spiritual-e-book.html

Jeftovic, Mark (2013). *The Tragedy Contrarianism*. Available: http://rebootingcapitalism.com/2013/03/05/the-tragedy-of-contrarianism/. Last accessed 12th September 2015.

Josephson, Michael (2012). Commentary 778.3: The Parable of Brother Leo. Available: http://whatwillmatter.com/2012/06/commentary-778-3-brother-leo-servant-leadership/. Last accessed 31st August 2015.

Lee, Bruce (2007). *Wisdom of Yoda, Bruce Lee.* Available: https://st4rbux.wordpress.com/2007/08/08/wisdom-of-yoda-bruce-lee/. Last accessed 31st August 2015.

Lundstrom, M. (1996). *A Wink from the Cosmos*. Available: http://www. fl owpower.com/synchro.htm. Last accessed 4th Jan 2011.

M, Vishal. (2014). *The Elephant Who Lost An Eye.* Available: http://sociallifestyle.blogspot.com.au/2014/08/the-elephant-who-lost-eye.html Last accessed 26th August 2015.

Mali, Taylor. (2011). *What Teachers Makes*. Available: http://www.taylormali.com/?s=what+do+you+make&submit=Search Last accessed 2nd October 2015

Peterson, W.E. *Three red marbles*. Available: http://www.crossroad.to/Victory/stories/marbles.htm. Last accessed 25th August 2015.

Randolph, Keith. (2002). *Sports Visualizations*. Available: https://www.llewellyn.com/encyclopedia/article/244. Last accessed 2nd October 2015.

Reilly, Rick. *This is a human interest story. Be sure to watch the video at the end.* Excerpt from Sports Illustrated. Available: http://www.swcs.com.au/hoyts.htm. Last accessed 26th August 2015.

Saraswati, Swami Chidanand. (2004). *Guru Purnima Blessings from Pujya Swamiji* Available: http://www.ihrf.com/messages/guru-purnima2004.html. Last accessed: 12th September 2015

Shah, Idries. (1969). Tales of the Dervishes: Teaching-stories of the Sufi Masters over the past thousand years. Available: http://www.ratical.org/ratville/JFK/TalesOfTheDervishes.pdf. Last accessed: 2nd October 2015

Sureshlasi (2008). *One Minute Can Change A Life.* Available: http://www.cssforum.com.pk/off-topic-section/humorous-inspirational-general-stuff/16831-one-minute-can-change-life.html. Last accessed 12th September 2015

Sykes, Stephen Randolph. (2010) Best religion is the one that makes one better. Available: http://www.staradvertiser.com/columnists/20100703_best_religion_is_the_one_that_makes_one_better.html?id=97719389. Last accessed 4th September 2015.

Sylvia, C. (2008). *I was given a young man's heart - and started craving beer and Kentucky Fried Chicken. My daughter said I even walked like a man.* Available: http://www.dailymail.co.uk/health/article-558256/ . Last accessed 4th July 2000

The Emperor And The Seed. (2011). Available: http://islam.ru/en/content/story/emperor-and-seed. Last accessed 12th September 2015

The Hundredth Monkey Phenomenon. (2009). Available: http:// www. storiesofwisdom.com/the-hundredth-monkey-phenomenon/. Last accessed 4th May 2011.

Tugend, Alina. (2010). *Too Many Choices: A Problem That Can Paralyze.* Available: http://www.nytimes.com/2010/02/27/ your-money/27shortcuts.html?_r=1 Last accessed 12th September 2015.

Unknown. *On being human.* Available: http://www. hypnotherapy-nicolaseeman.co.uk/On-Being-Human.php. Last accessed 12th September 2015

Widemark, S. (2009). *Lessons From The Geese.* Available: http:// suewidemark.com/lessonsgeese.htm. Last accessed 20th Dec 2011.

Yarow, Jay. (2011). *The Full Text Of Steve Jobs' Stanford Commencement Speech.* Available: http://www. businessinsider.com.au/the-full-text-of-steve-jobs-stanford-commencement-speech-2011-10. Last accessed 4th August 2015.

Audio

Tracy, Brian (1993). *Maximum Achievement.* Simon & Schuster Audio

CPSIA information can be obtained
at www.ICGtesting.com
Printed in the USA
BVHW071829140119
537782BV00002B/194/P